DAVID SHESKIN's

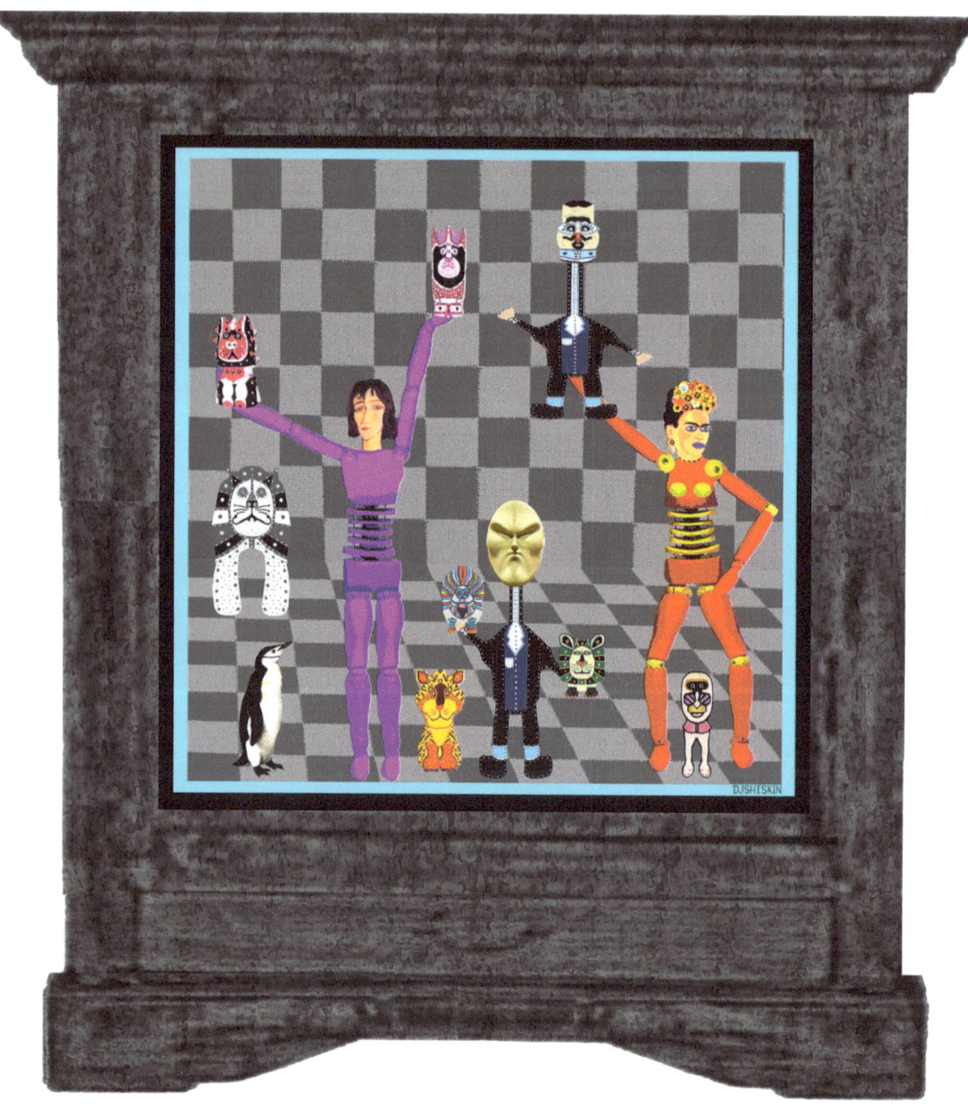

CABINET OF CURIOSITIES

David Sheskin's Cabinets of Curiosities

Published in the United States and the United Kingdom
by WingSpan Press, Livermore, CA

ISBN 978-1-63683-026-1 (pbk.)
ISBN 978-1-63683-977-6 (ebk.)

First edition 2022

Printed in the United States of America

www.wingspanpress.com

Library of Congress Control Number: 2021925007

1 2 3 4 5 6 7 8 9 10

Table of Contents

Introduction

All members of the general public, especially those who are serious collectors of fine art and antiquities, are cordially invited to view *David Sheskin's Cabinets of Curiosities*. During the next two years all or part of the collection contained in this catalogue is scheduled to be displayed in the Metropolitan Museum of Art in New York, the Louvre Museum in Paris, the Tokyo National Museum and The National Museum of China in Beijing. At some point in the foreseeable future it is anticipated that selected works from the collection will be made available for purchase by museums, philanthropic institutions, Fortune 500 companies and members of the general public. Interested parties may submit bids for any of the cabinets (or objects displayed within) to the curator of *David Sheskin's Cabinets of Curiosities* at the collection website. Upon request the curator will provide prospective buyers with specific details (e.g., dimensions, media employed, etc.) regarding the contents of each cabinet. Since the contents of some cabinets are permanent installations, the latter type of cabinet may only be purchased intact. All bids (which will be kept strictly confidential) should identify the number of the cabinet one is interested in purchasing or the placement of any object of interest within a cabinet (i.e., U: Upper; Lo: Lower; L: Left; R: Right; M: Middle). At a point in time to be determined by the collection curator, but no later than five years after the copyright date on this catalogue, whatever objects remain in the collection will be donated to the Museum of Antiquities and Curiosities which is presently under construction on Easter Island.

1: Cabinets Containing Guardians and Companions

The painted icons displayed in these cabinets are carved or sculpted from wood or stone. They are small enough in size to be kept in one's possession at all times. The artist refers to these icons as *Guardians* **and** *Companions***. A** *Guardian* **is an object intended to accompany and protect one in the afterlife, while a** *Companion* **is an object one should always keep in his or her possession for emotional support and to infuse one with courage.**

Cabinet 1

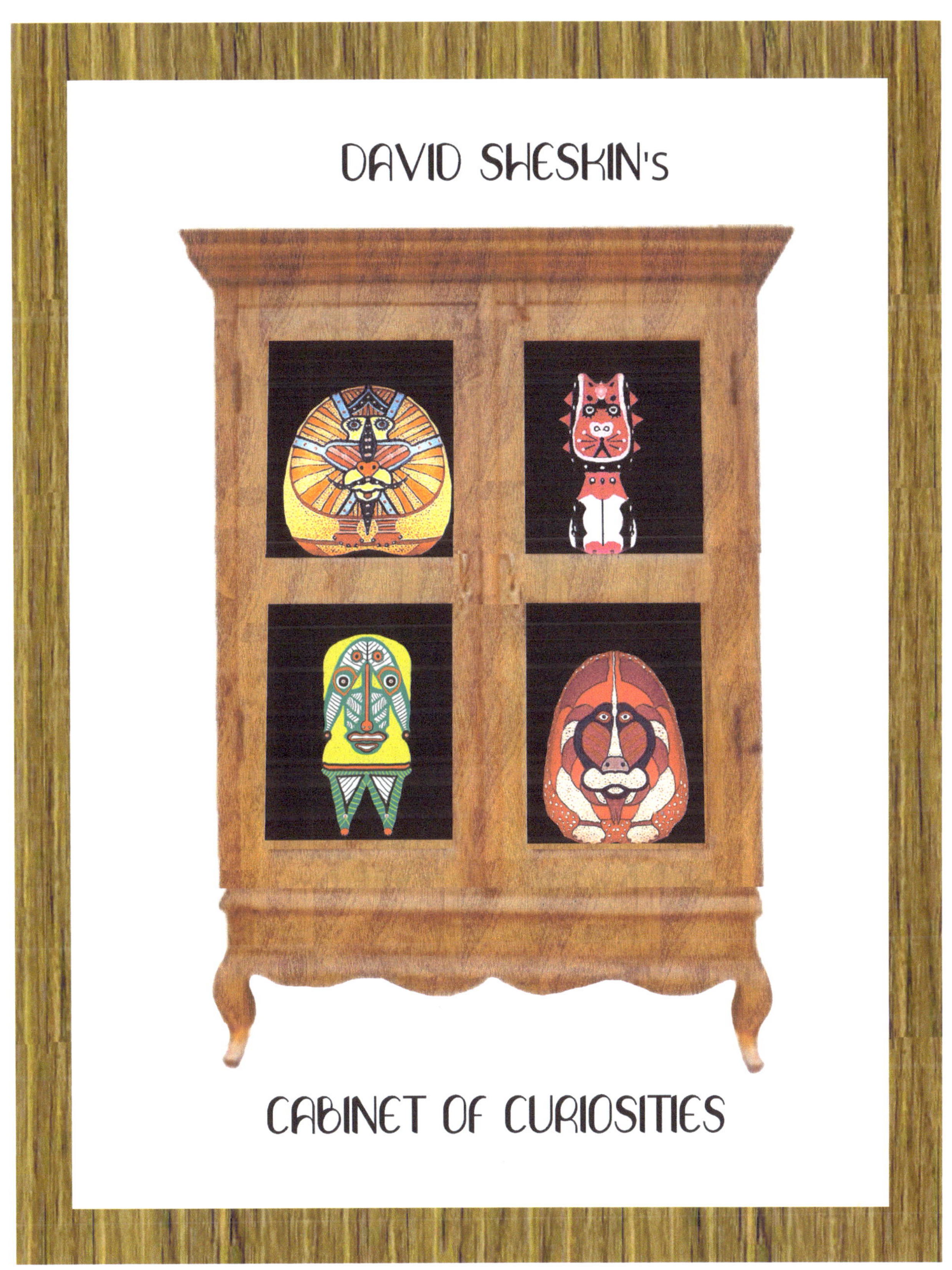
DAVID SHESKIN's
CABINET OF CURIOSITIES

Cabinet 2

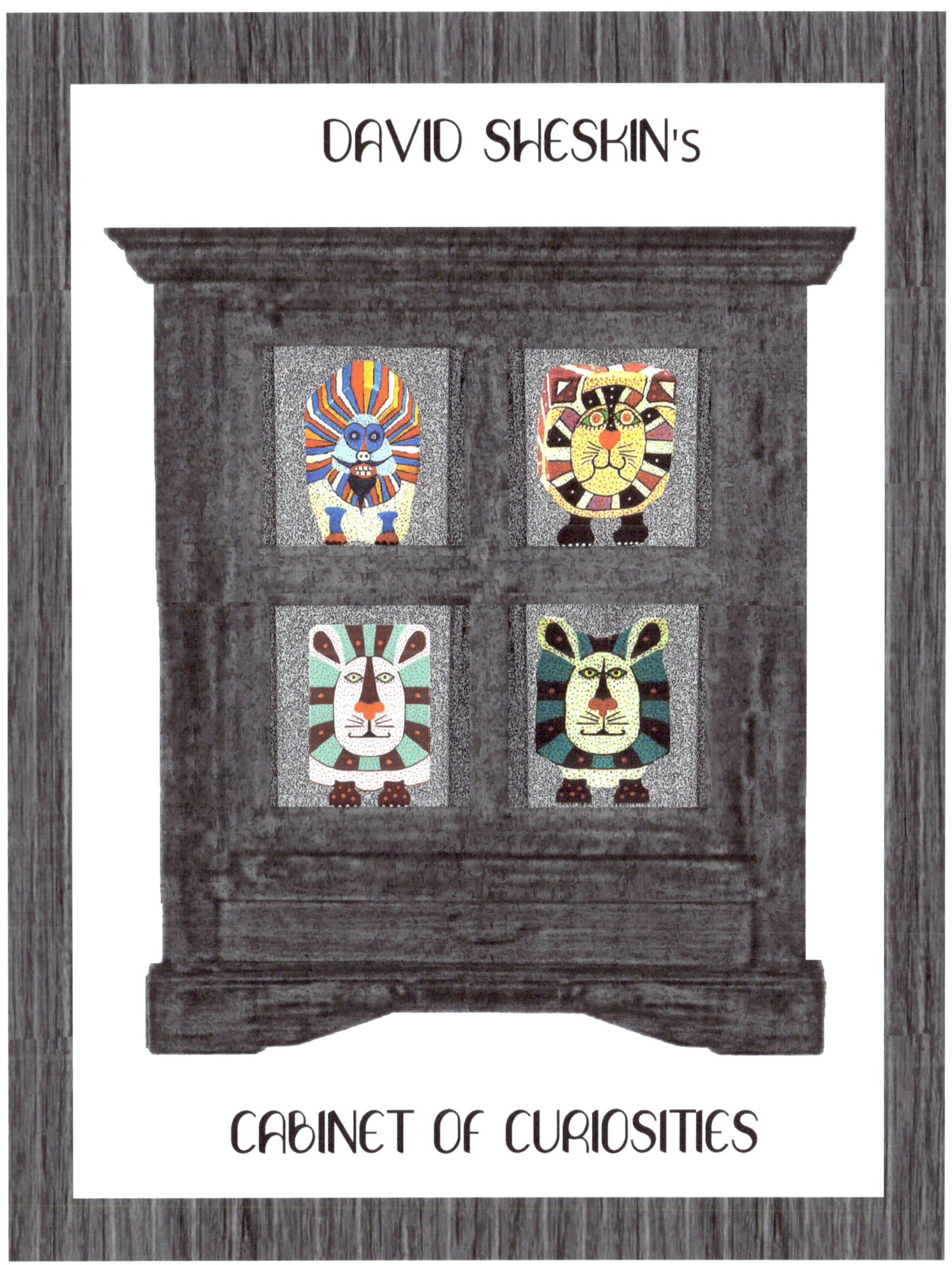
DAVID SHESKIN's
CABINET OF CURIOSITIES

Cabinet 3

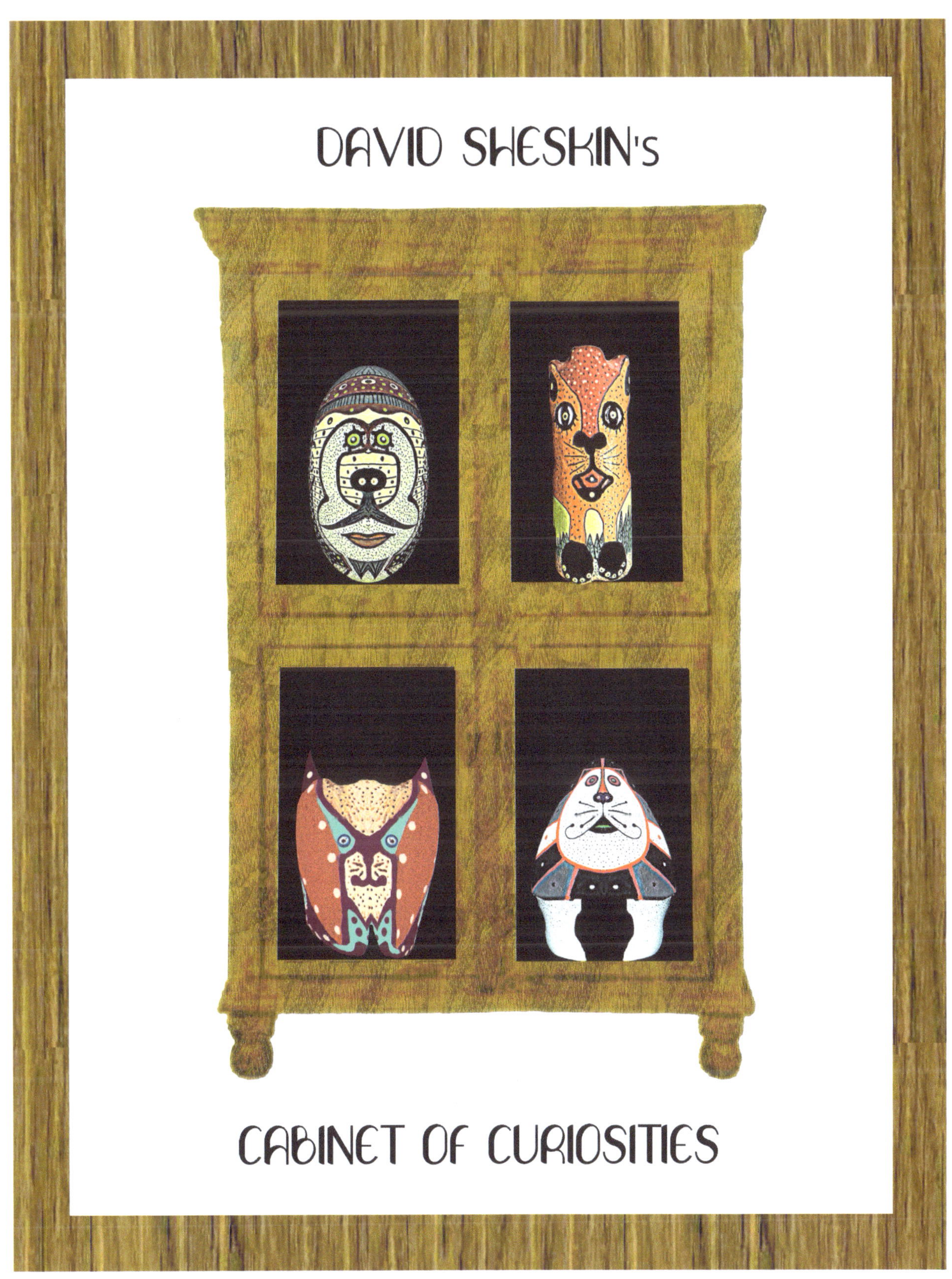
DAVID SHESKIN's
CABINET OF CURIOSITIES

Cabinet 4

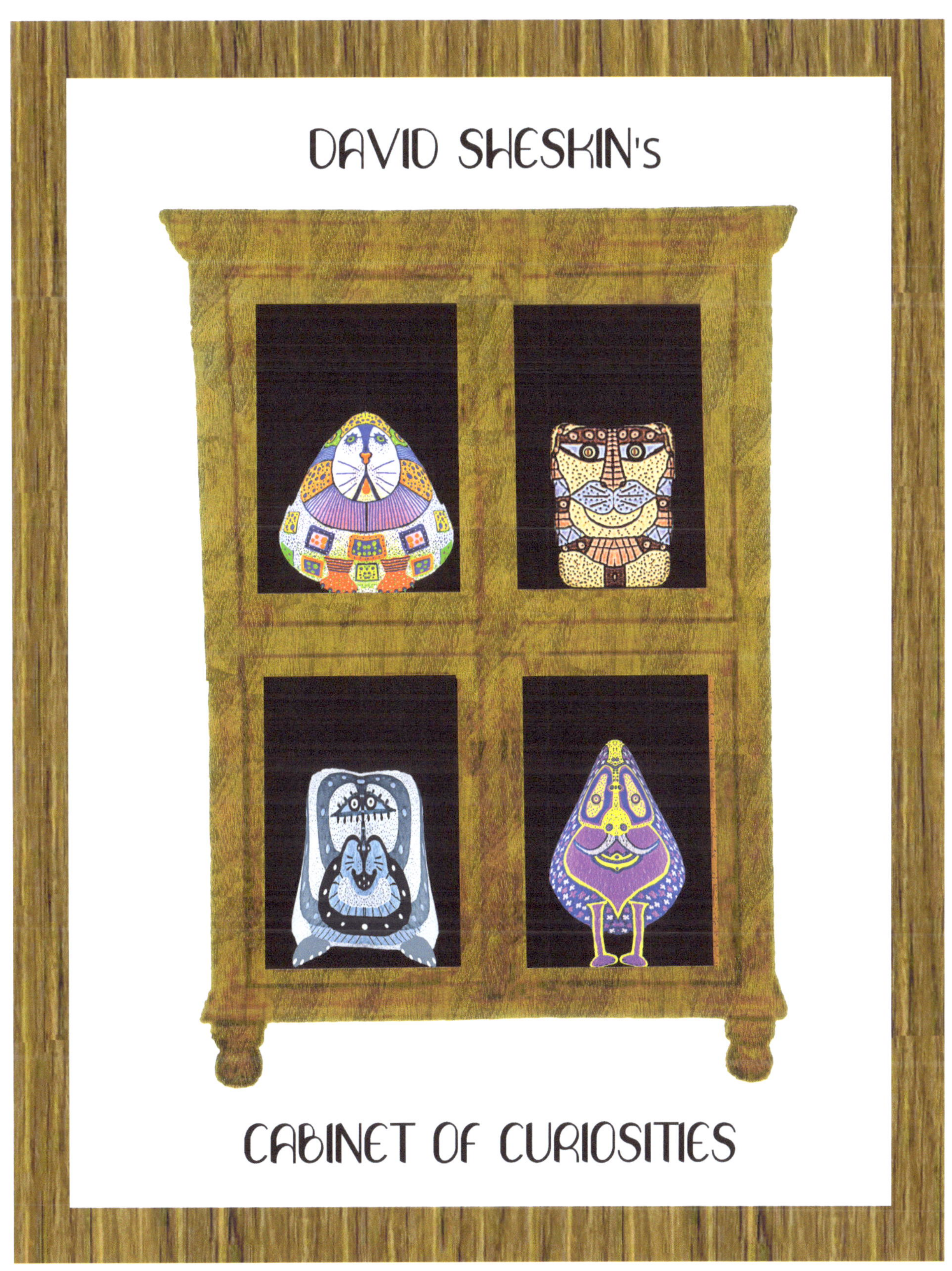
DAVID SHESKIN's
CABINET OF CURIOSITIES

Cabinet 5

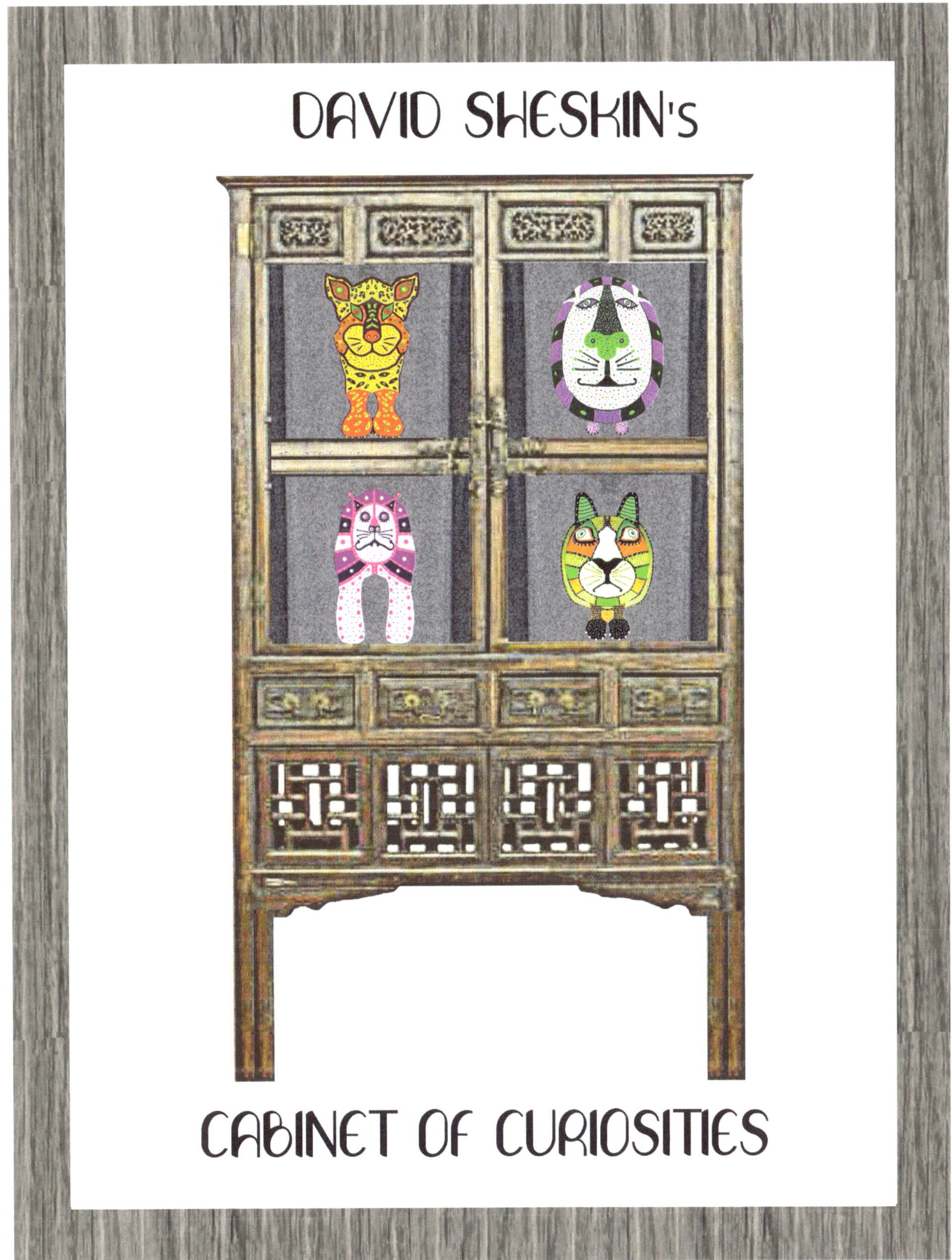
DAVID SHESKIN's
CABINET OF CURIOSITIES

Cabinet 6

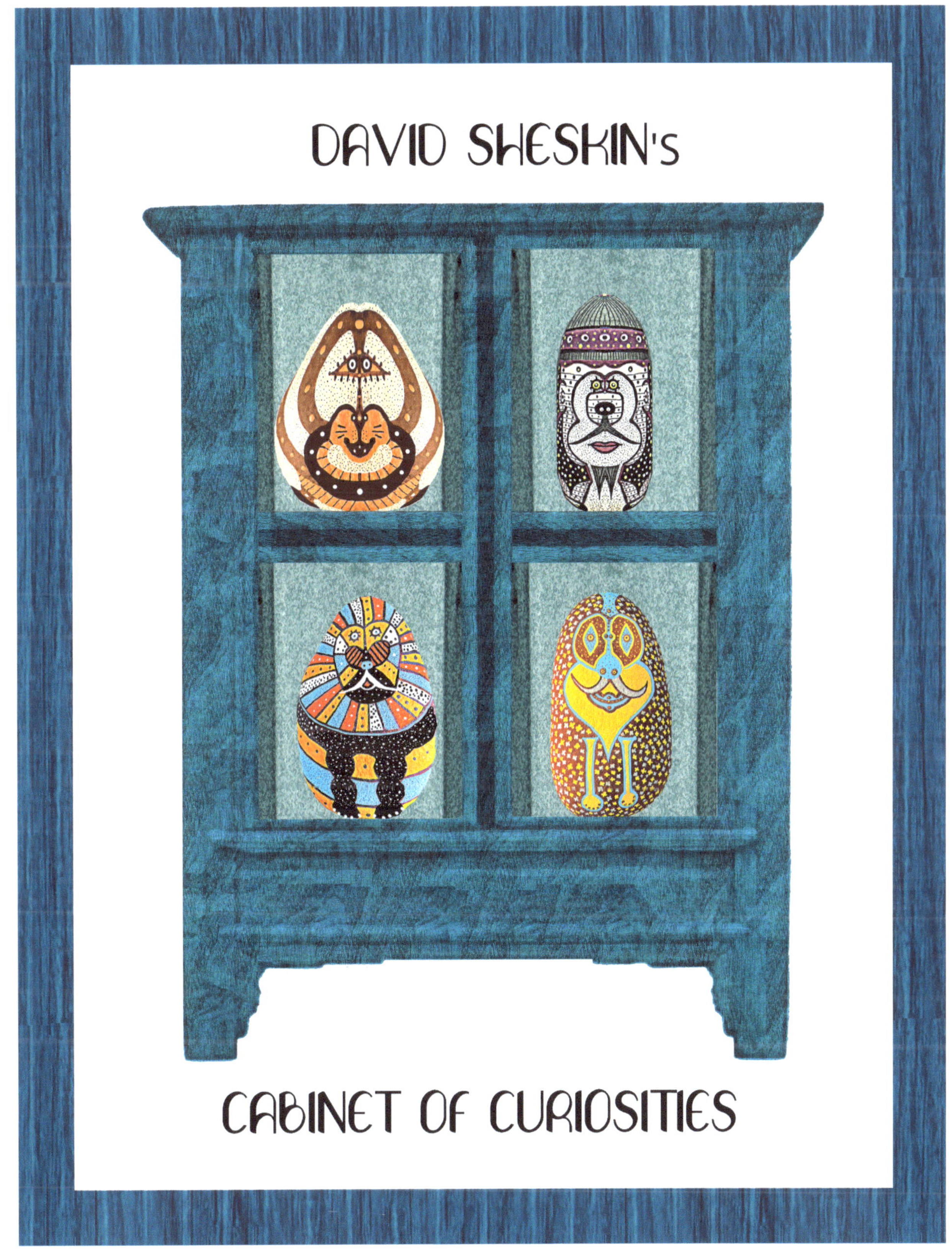
DAVID SHESKIN's
CABINET OF CURIOSITIES

Cabinet 7

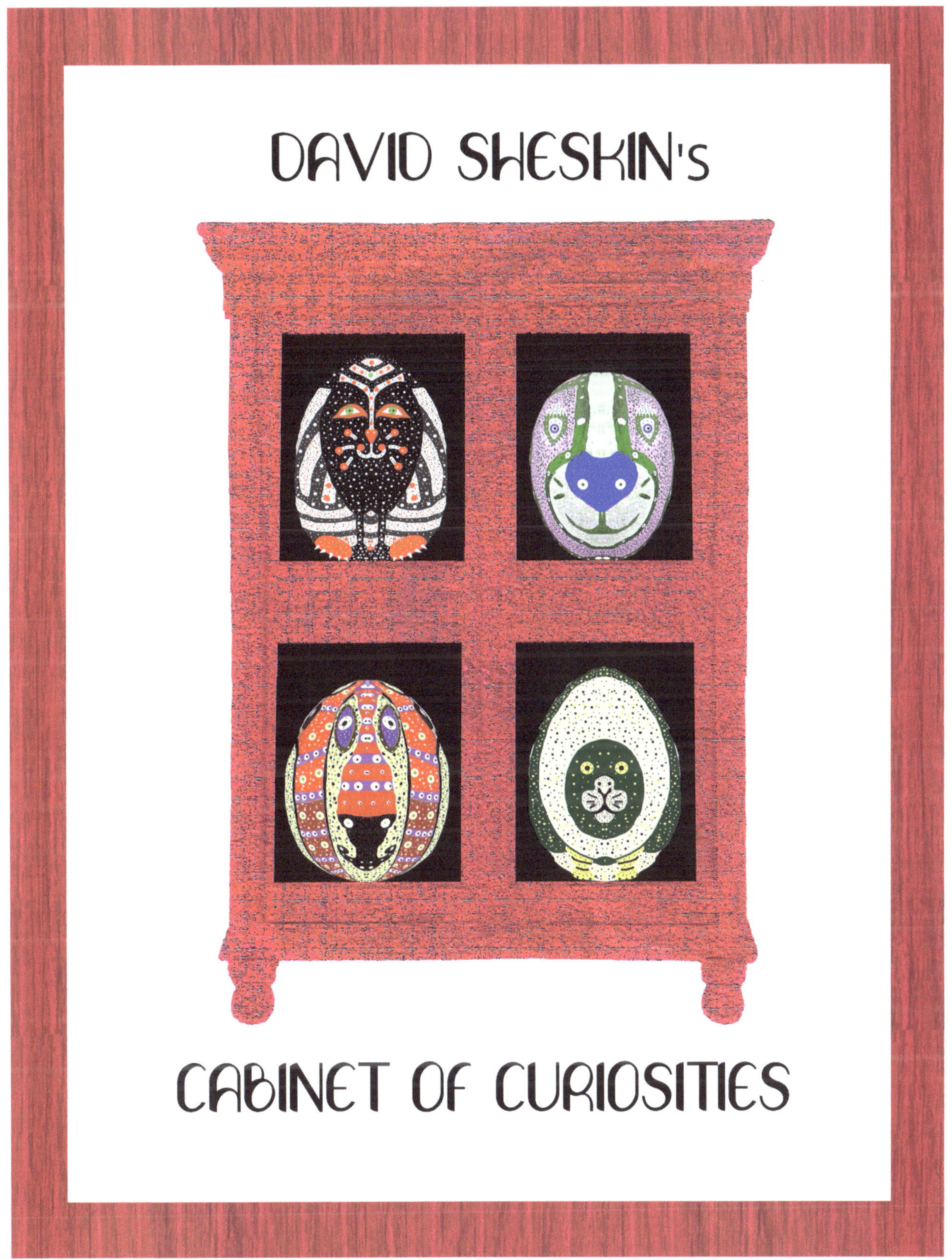
DAVID SHESKIN's
CABINET OF CURIOSITIES

Cabinet 8

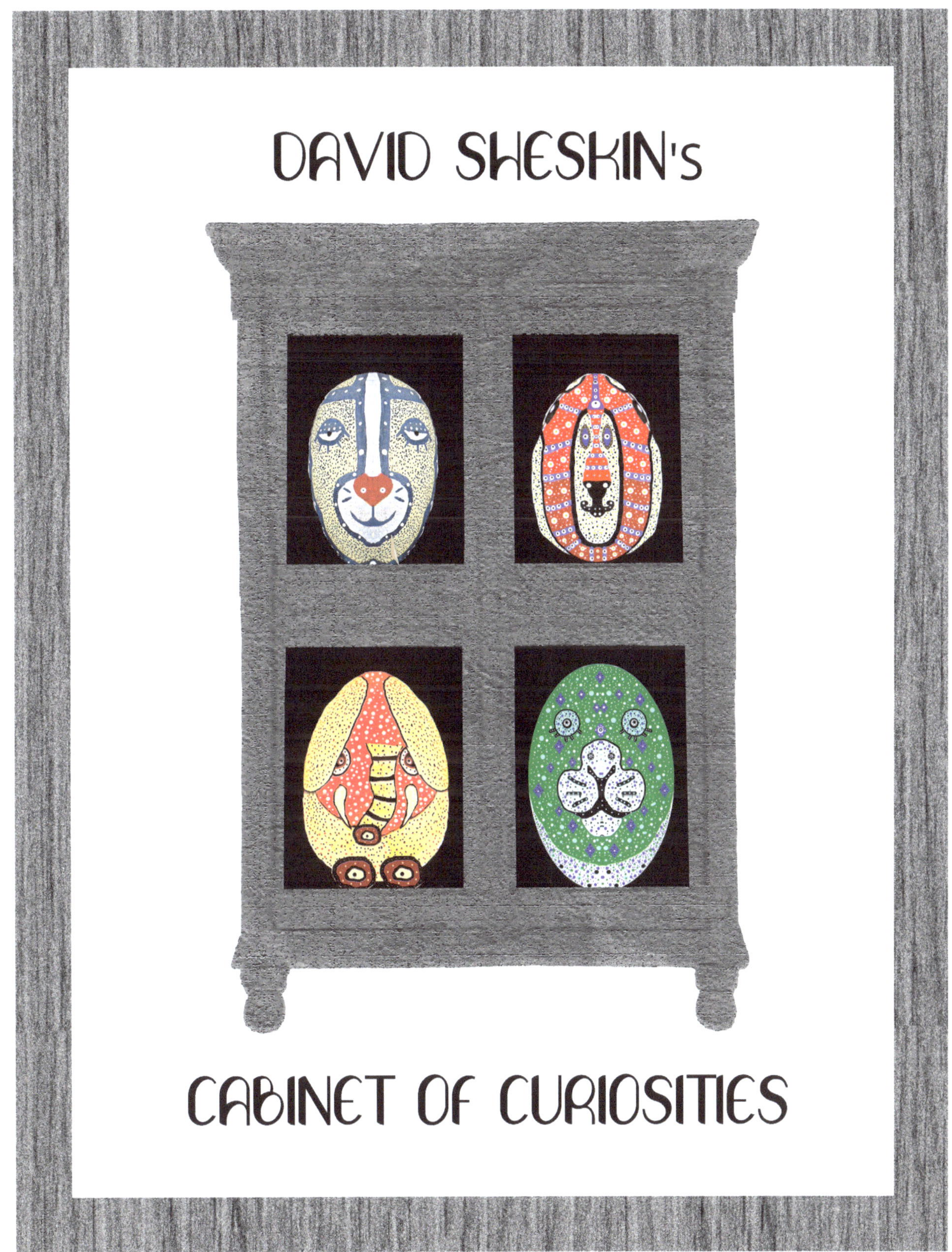
DAVID SHESKIN's
CABINET OF CURIOSITIES

Cabinet 9

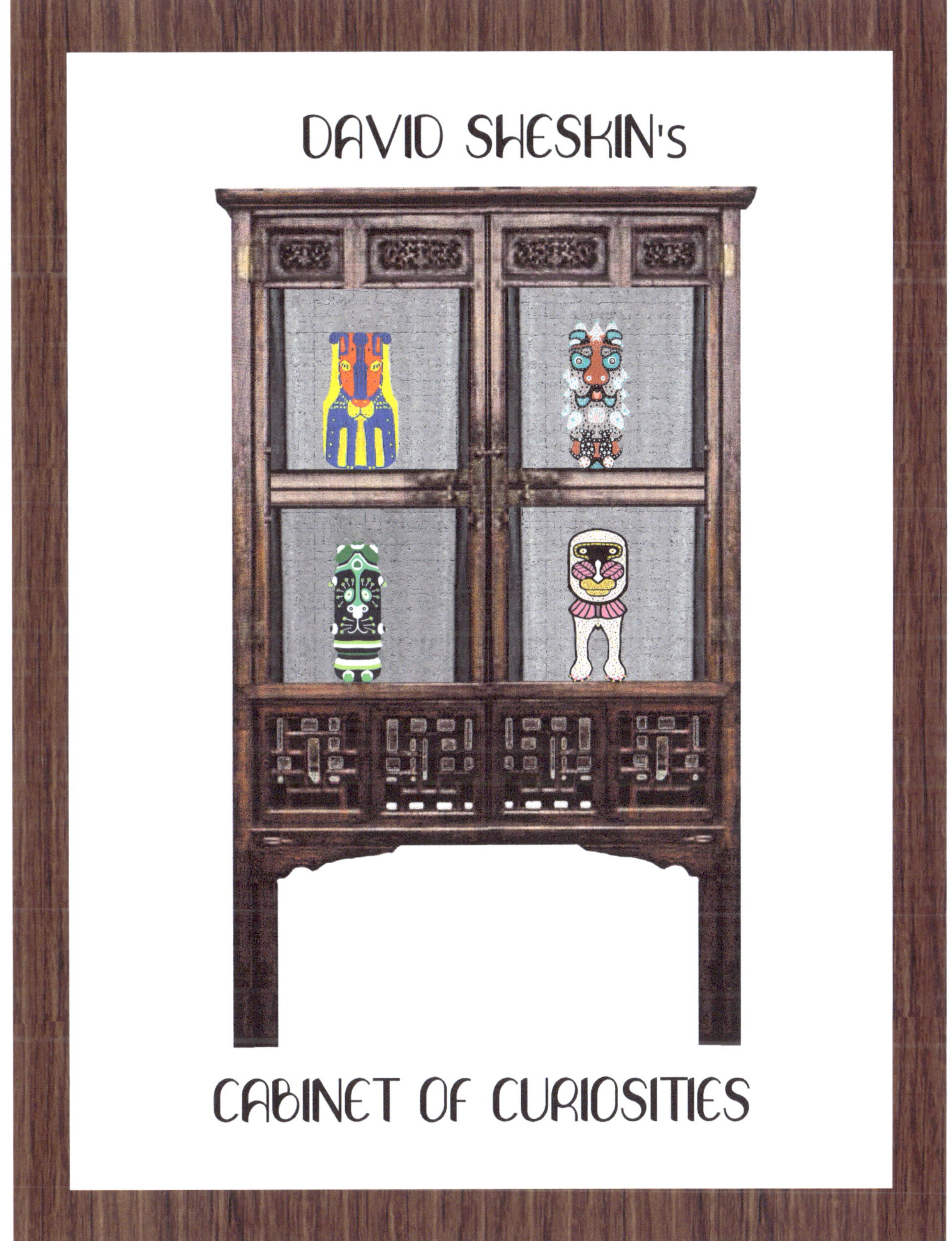
DAVID SHESKIN's
CABINET OF CURIOSITIES

Cabinet 10

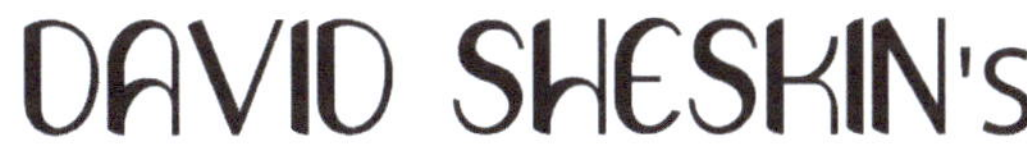

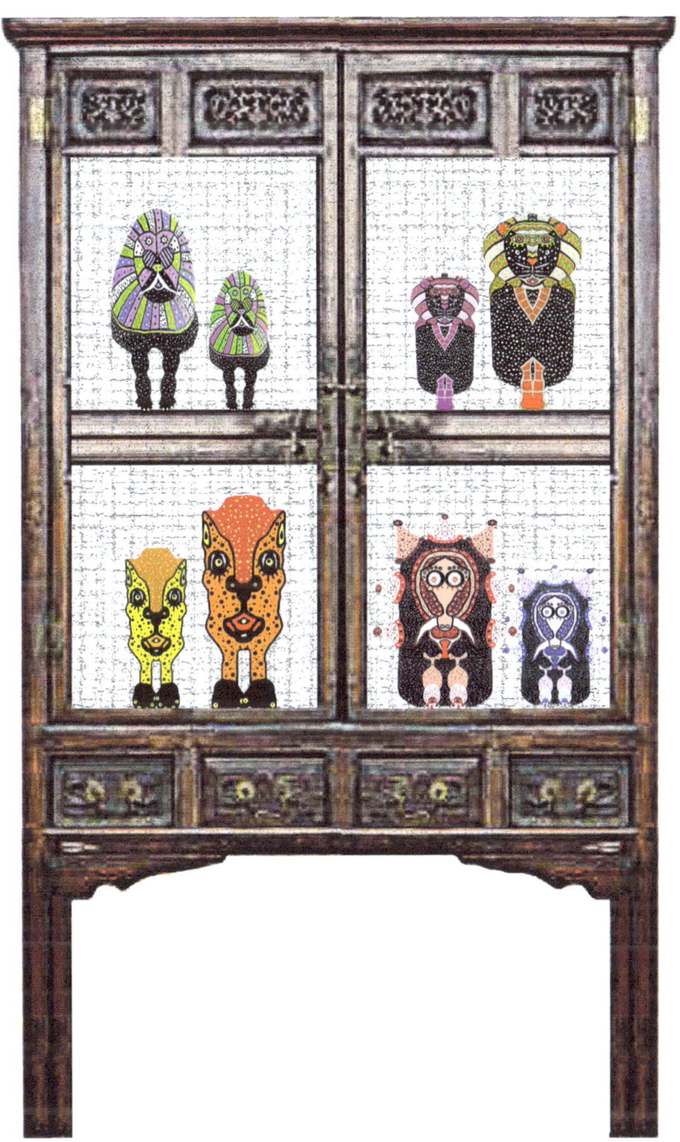

CABINET OF CURIOSITIES

Cabinet 11

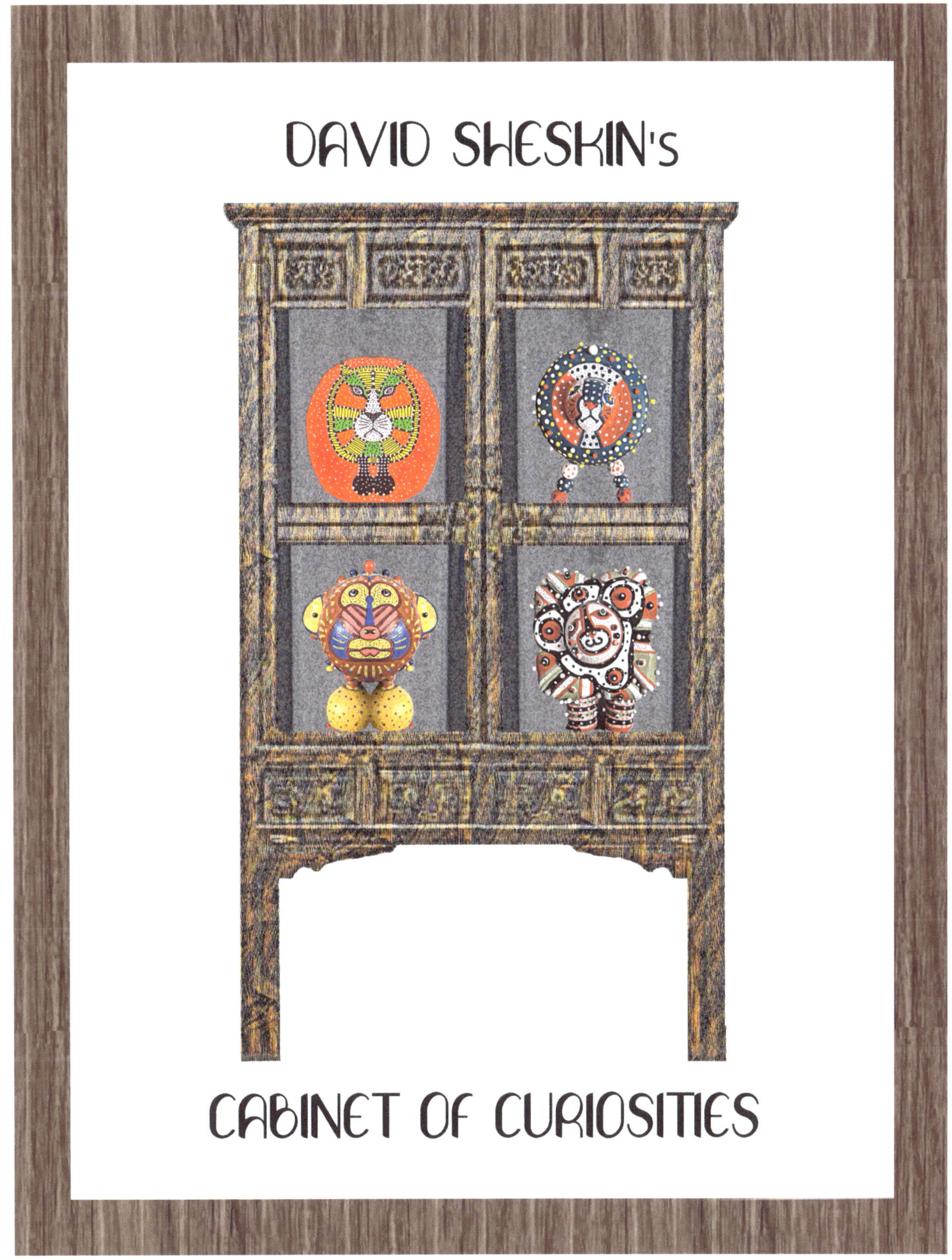
DAVID SHESKIN's
CABINET OF CURIOSITIES

Cabinet 12

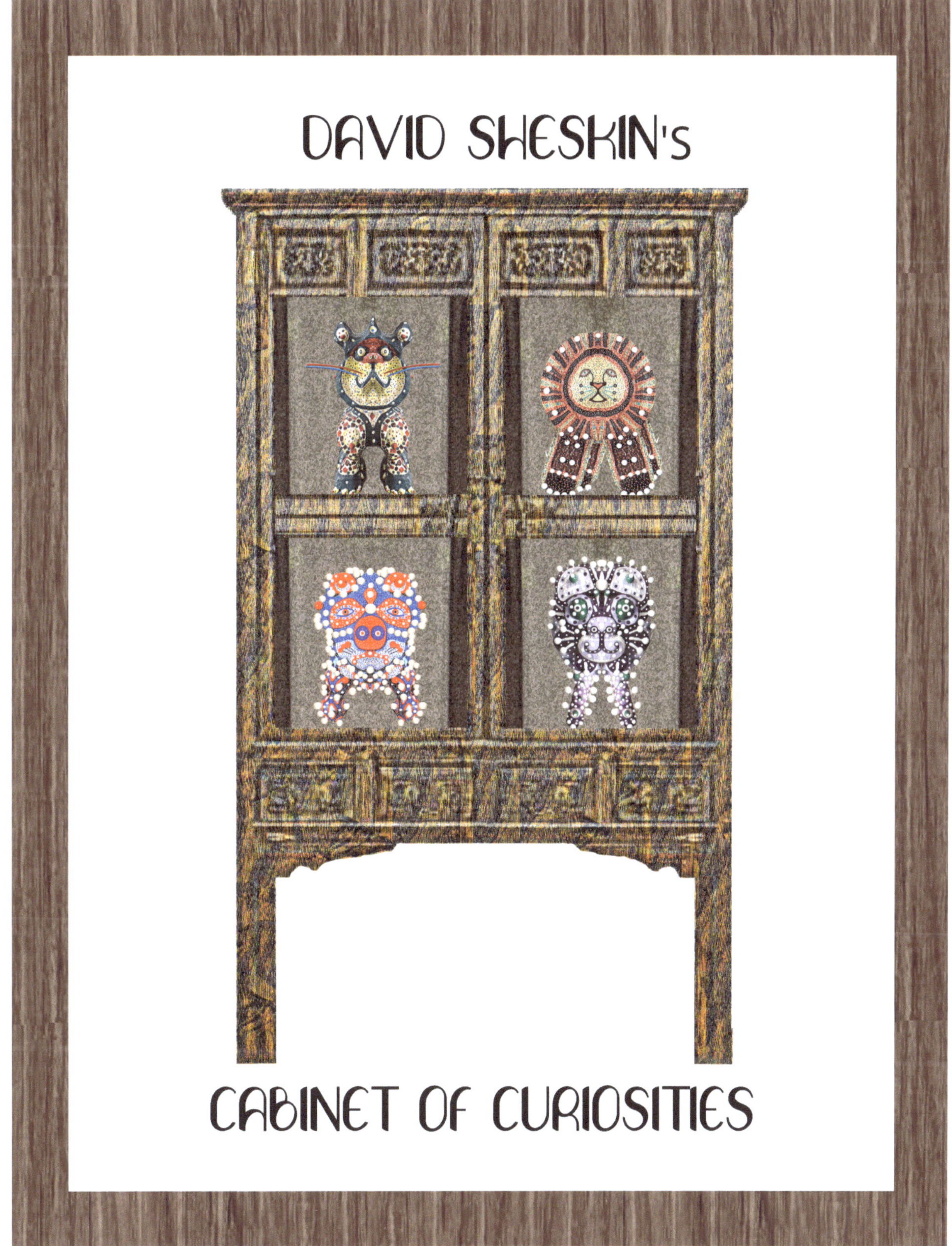
DAVID SHESKIN's
CABINET OF CURIOSITIES

Cabinet 13

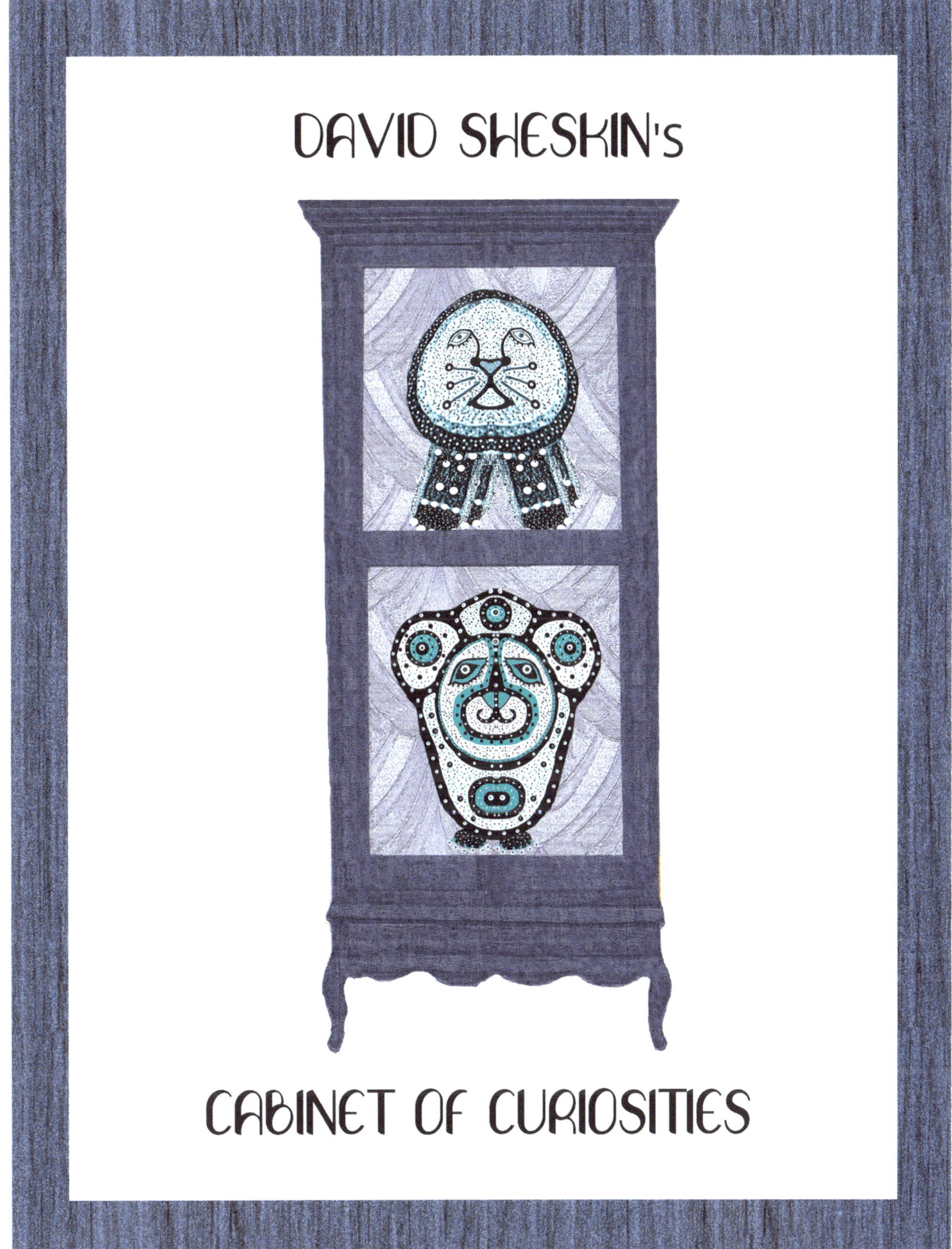
DAVID SHESKIN's
CABINET OF CURIOSITIES

Cabinet 14

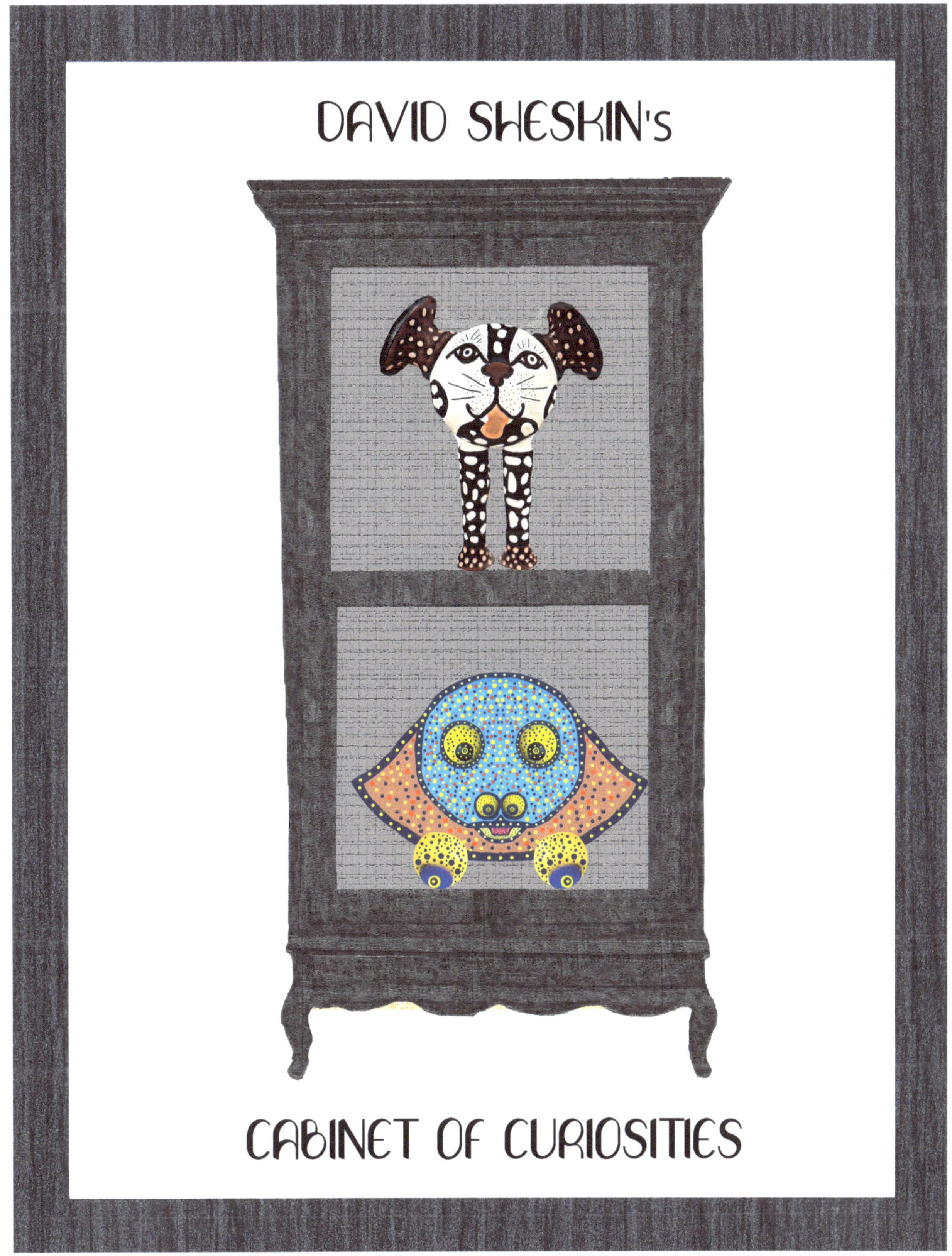
DAVID SHESKIN's
CABINET OF CURIOSITIES

Cabinet 15

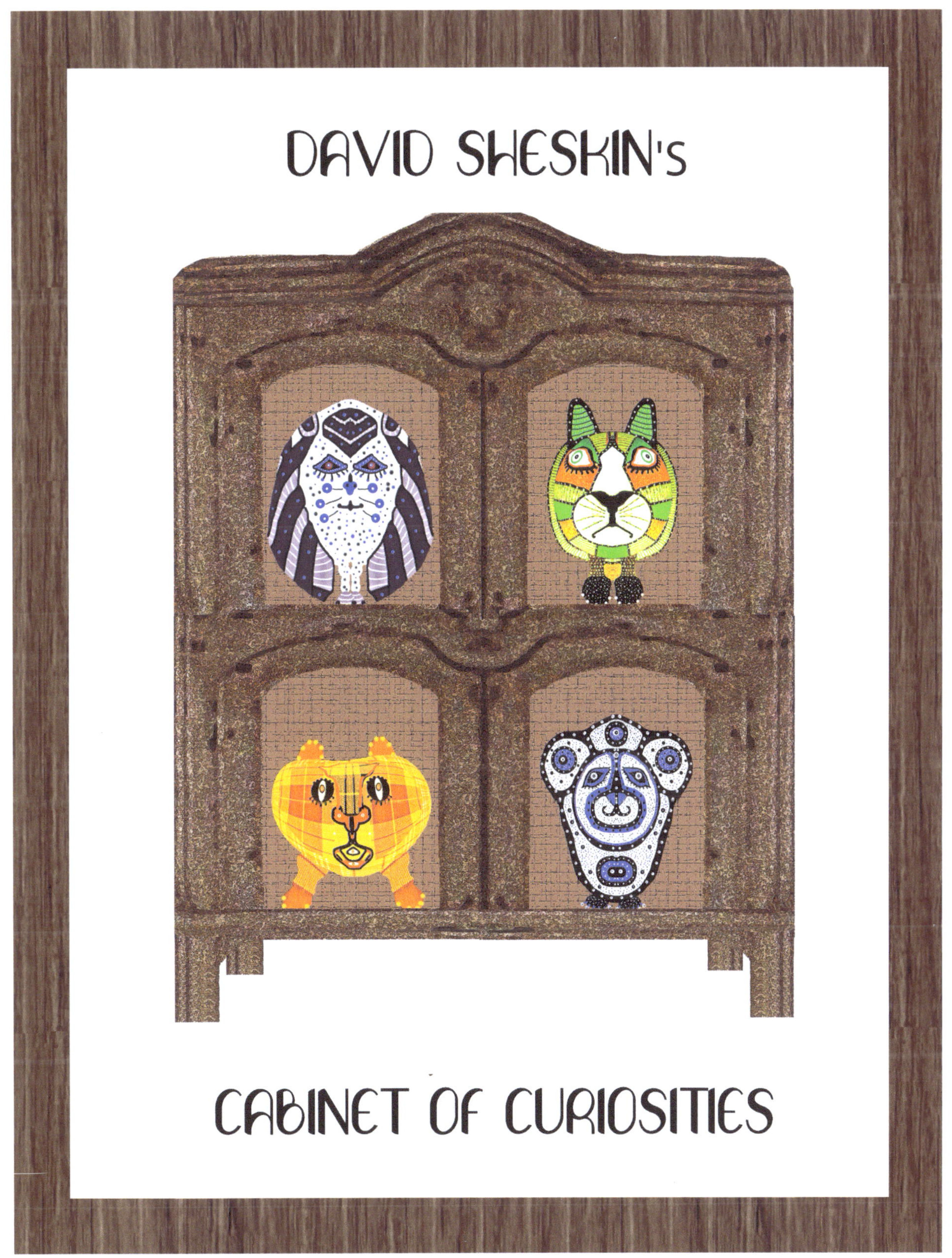
DAVID SHESKIN's
CABINET OF CURIOSITIES

Cabinet 16

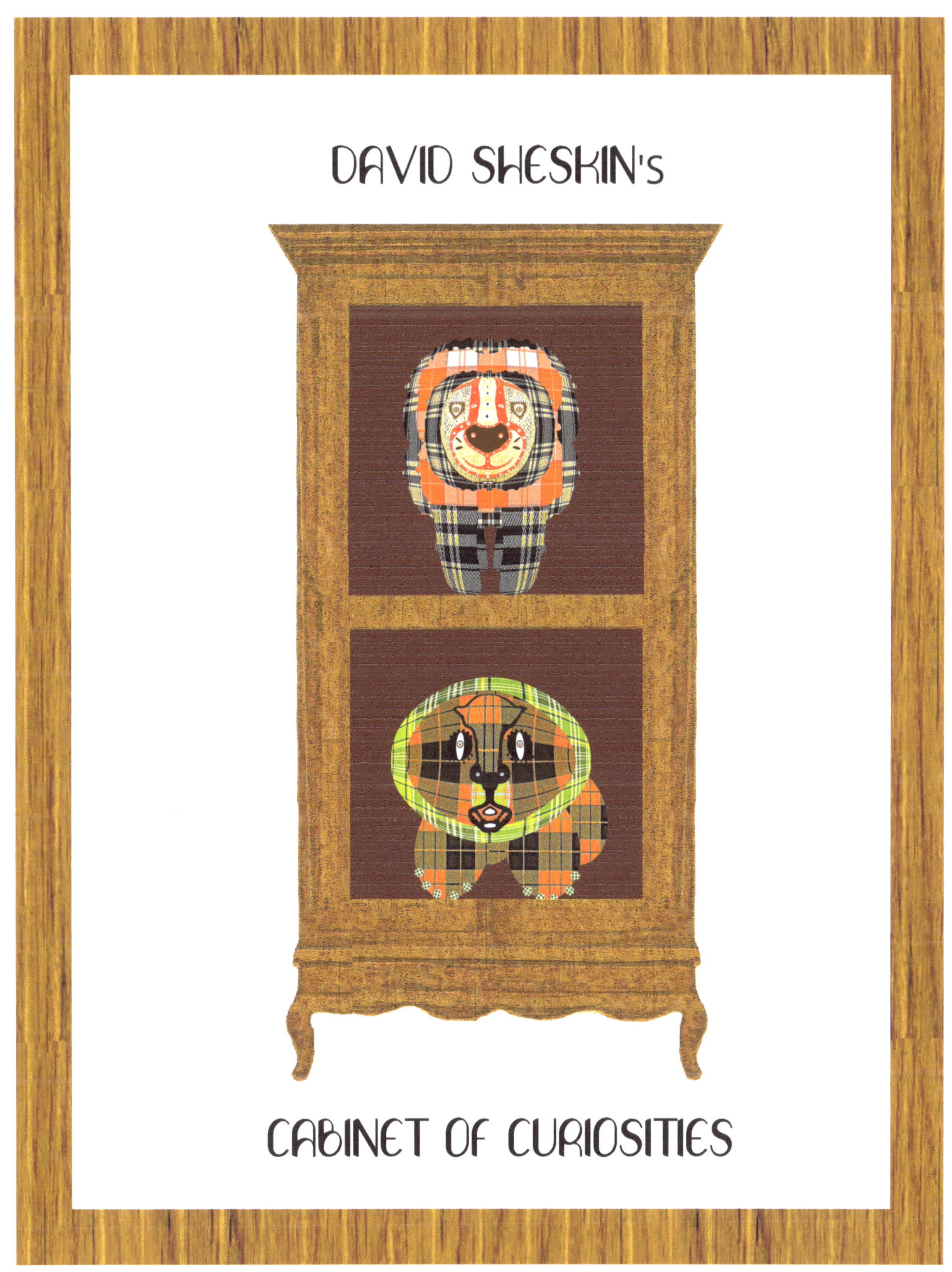
DAVID SHESKIN's
CABINET OF CURIOSITIES

Cabinet 17

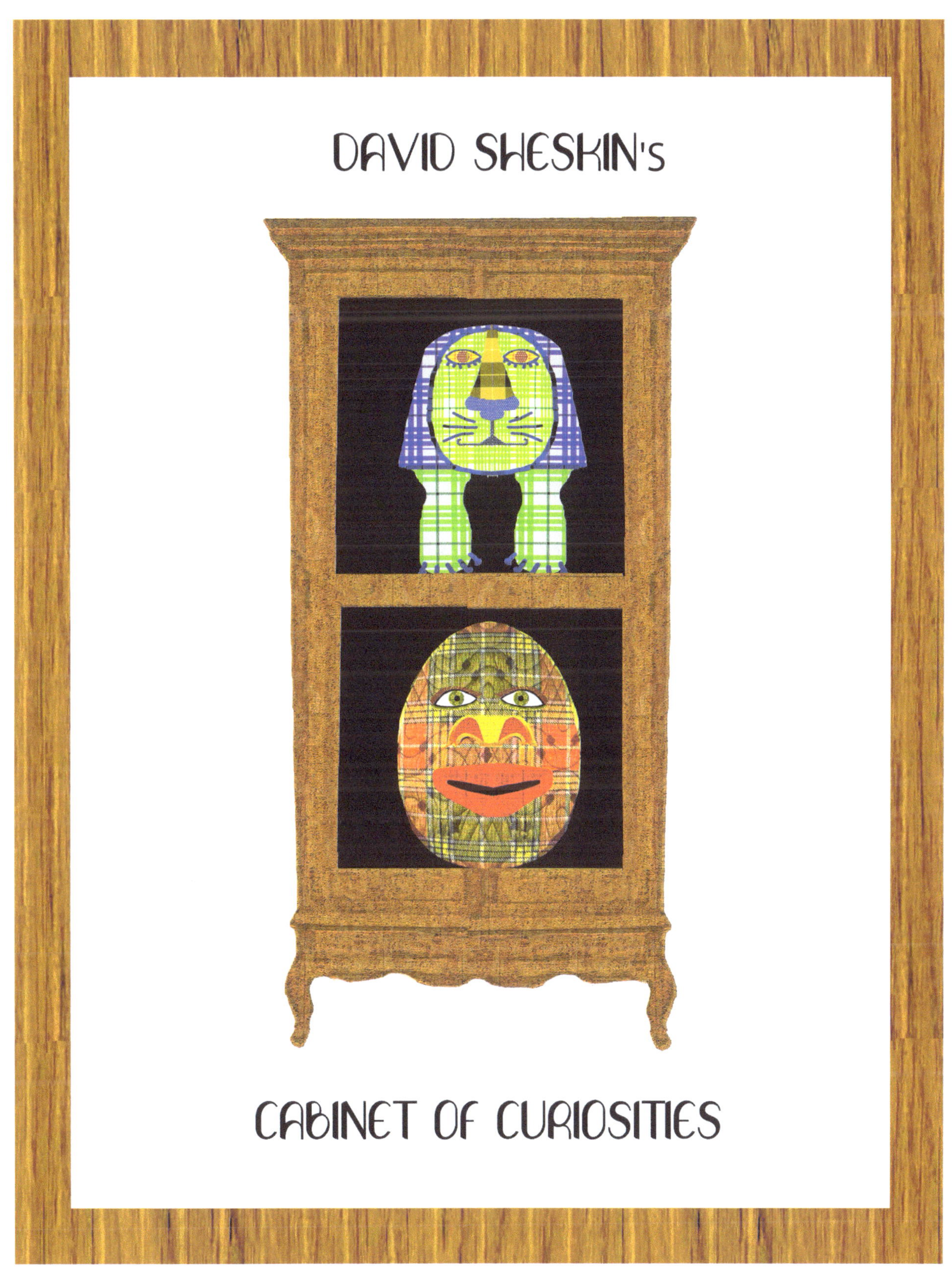
DAVID SHESKIN's
CABINET OF CURIOSITIES

Cabinet 18

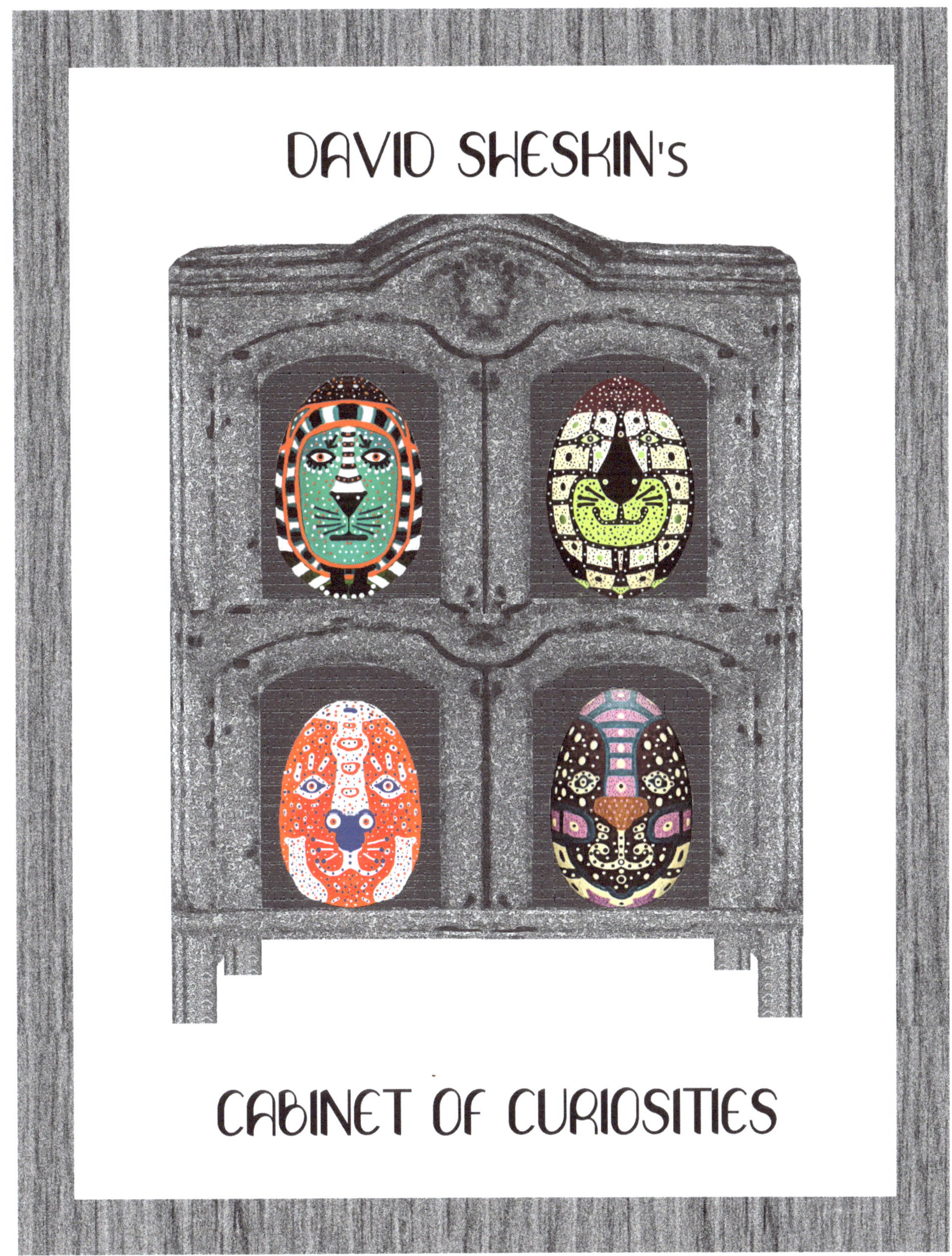
DAVID SHESKIN's
CABINET OF CURIOSITIES

Cabinet 19

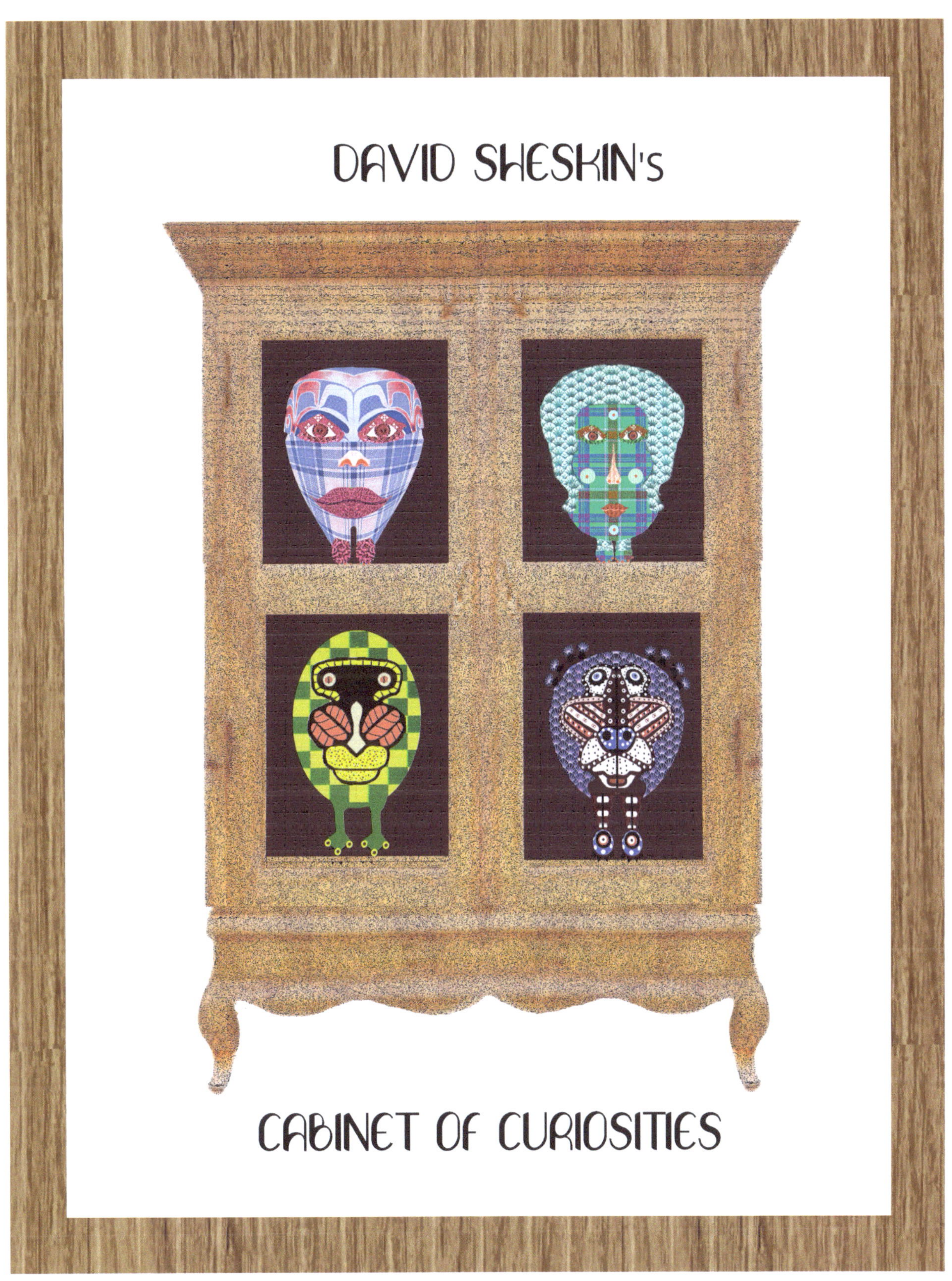
DAVID SHESKIN's
CABINET OF CURIOSITIES

Cabinet 20

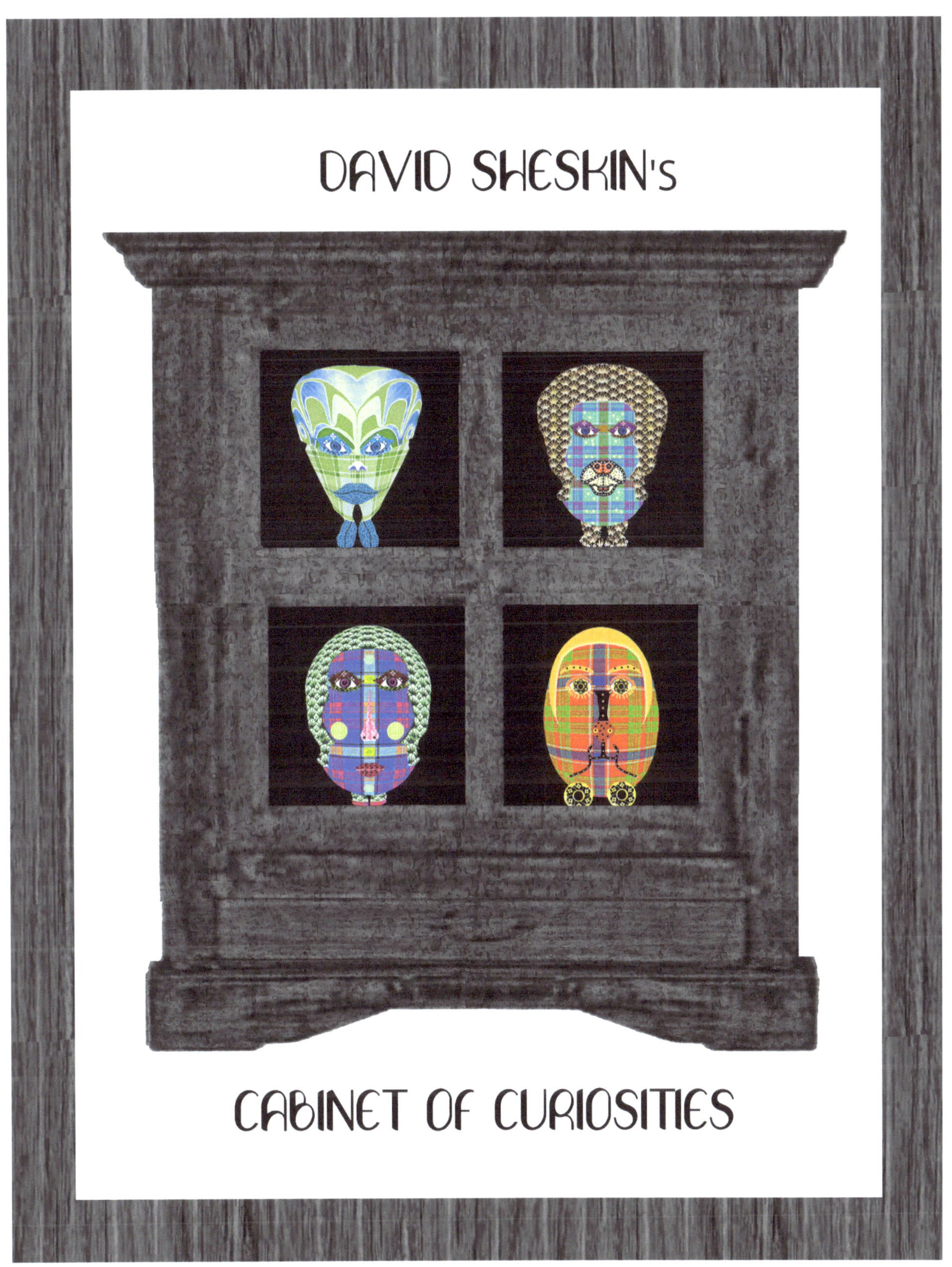
DAVID SHESKIN's
CABINET OF CURIOSITIES

Cabinet 21

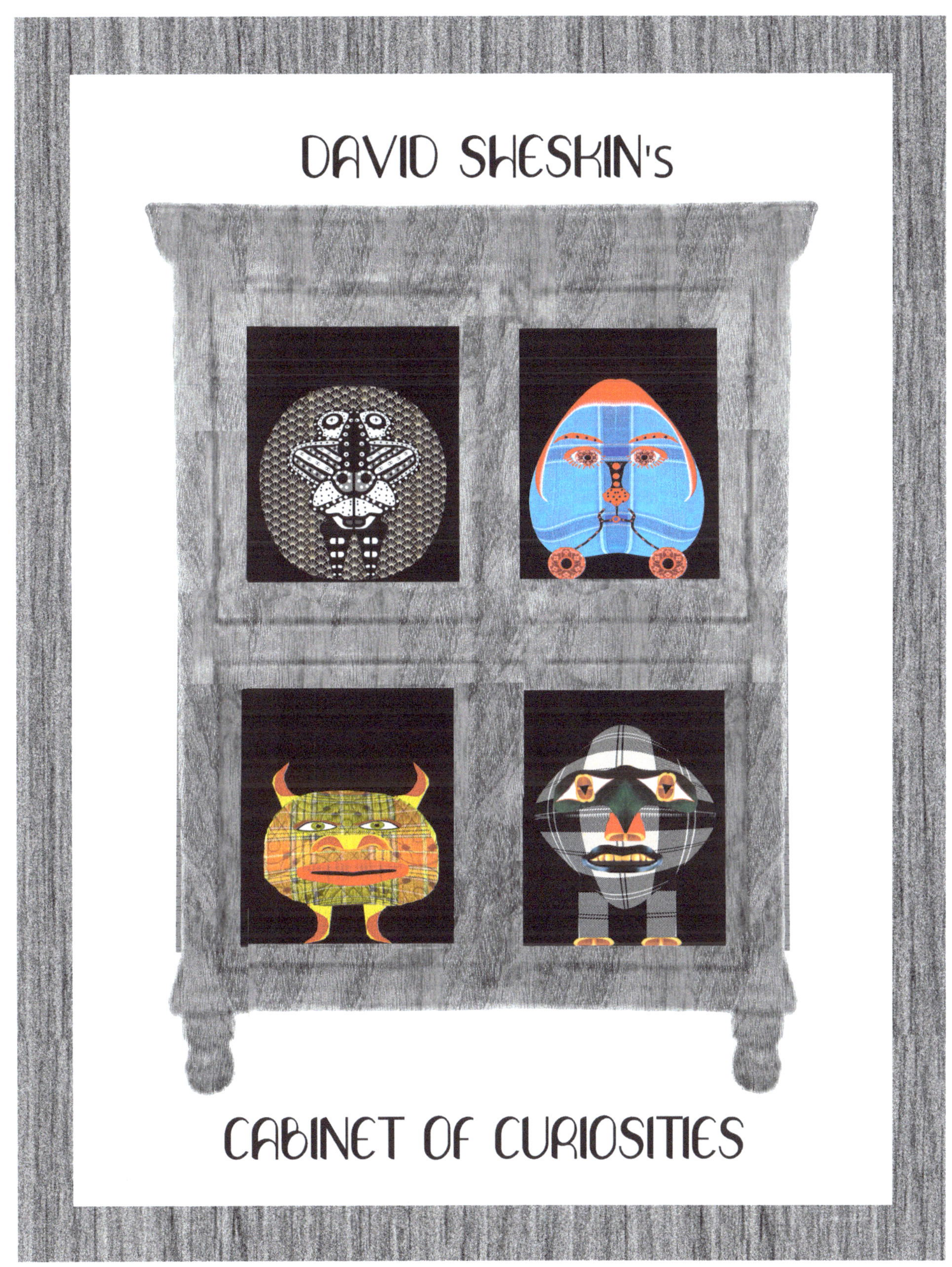
DAVID SHESKIN's
CABINET OF CURIOSITIES

Cabinet 22

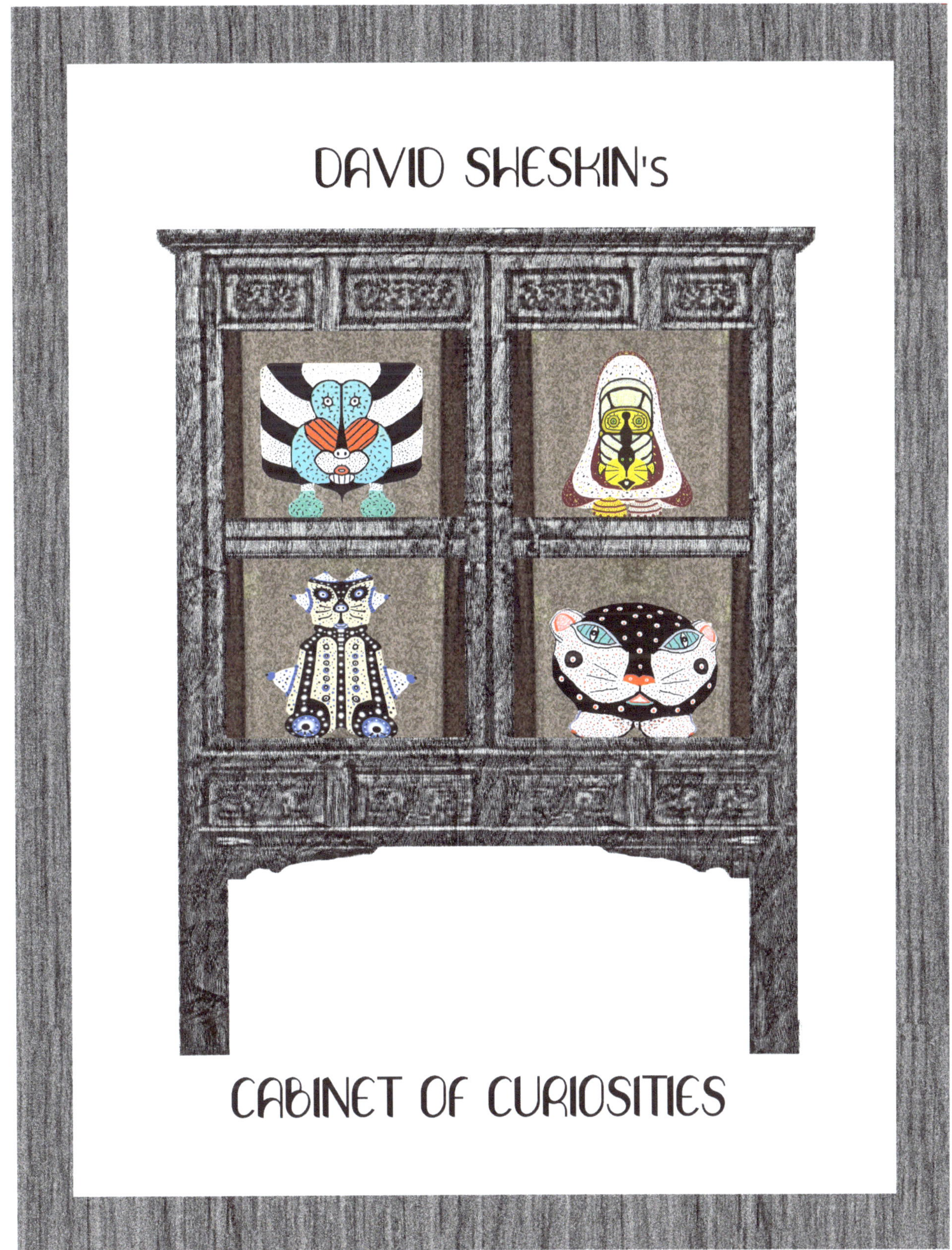
DAVID SHESKIN's
CABINET OF CURIOSITIES

Cabinet 23

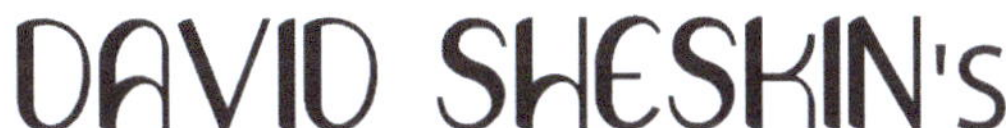

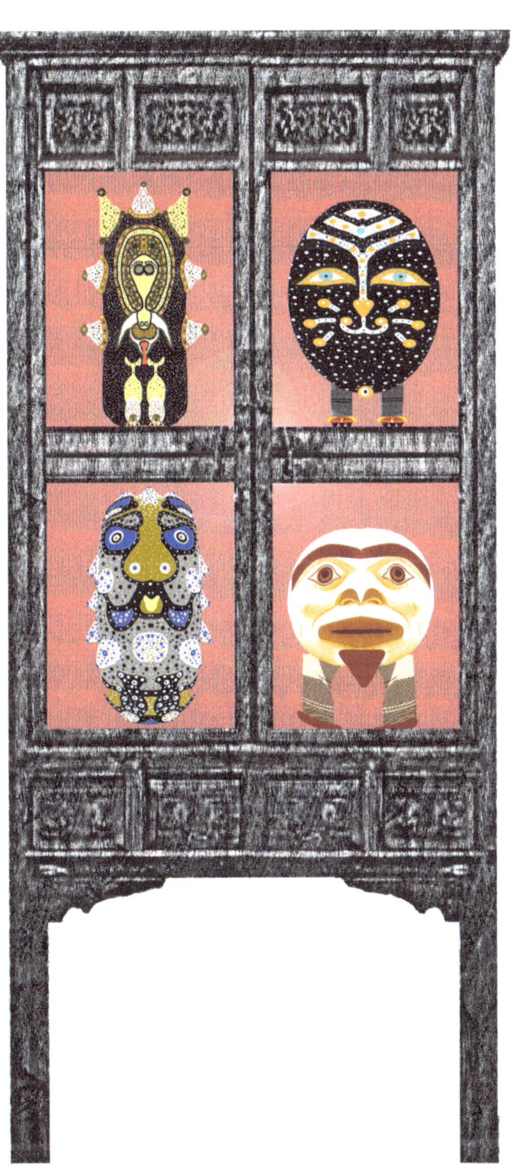

CABINET OF CURIOSITIES

Cabinet 24

DAVID SHESKIN's

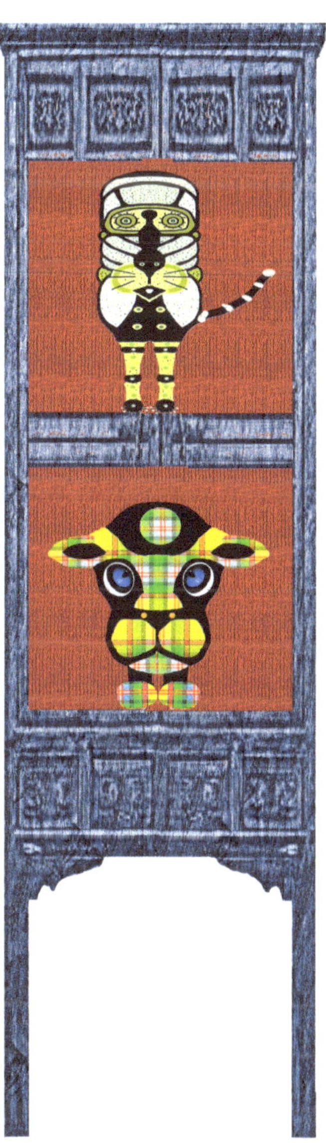

CABINET OF CURIOSITIES

Cabinet 25

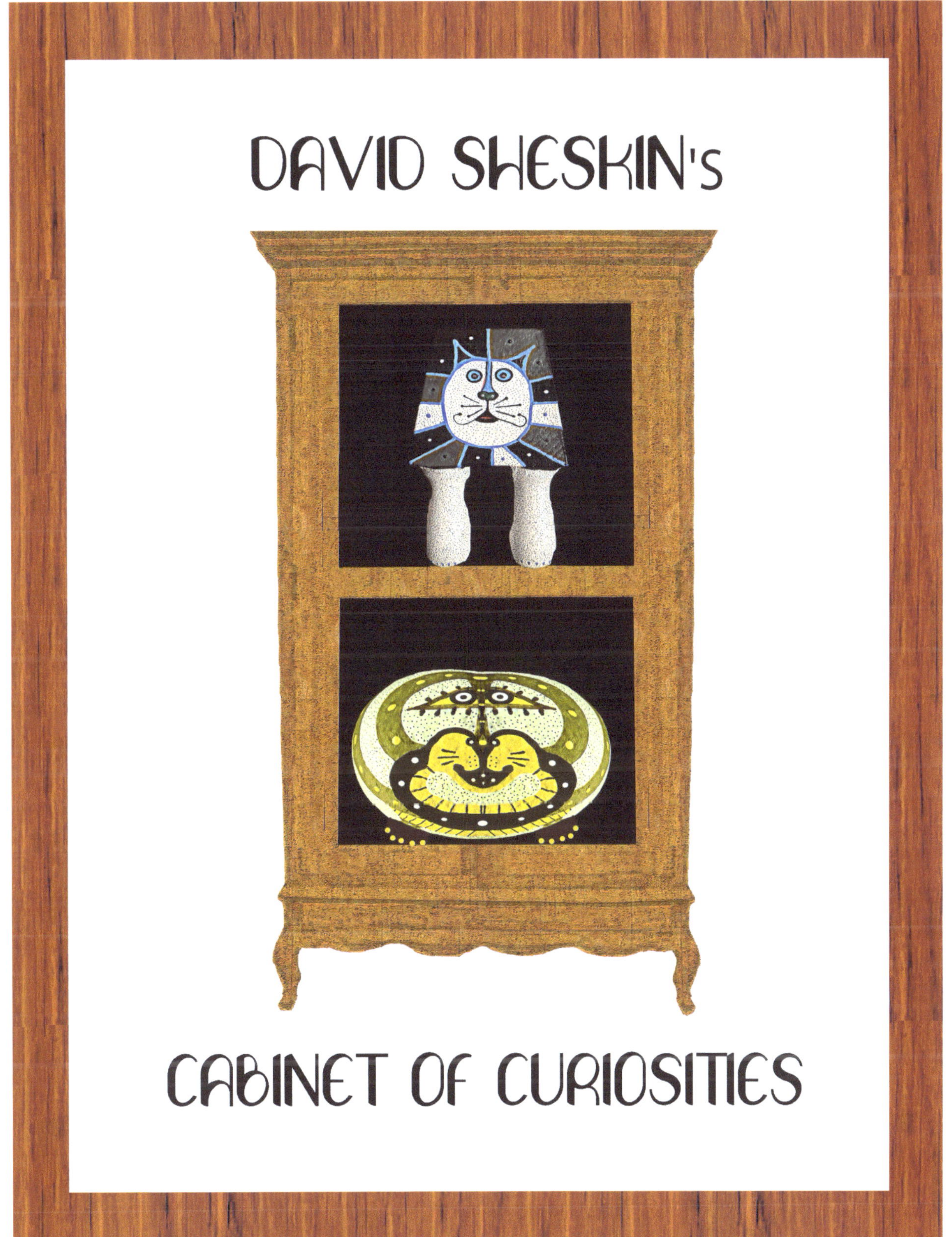
DAVID SHESKIN's
CABINET OF CURIOSITIES

2: Cabinets Containing Assorted Curiosities

Cabinet 26

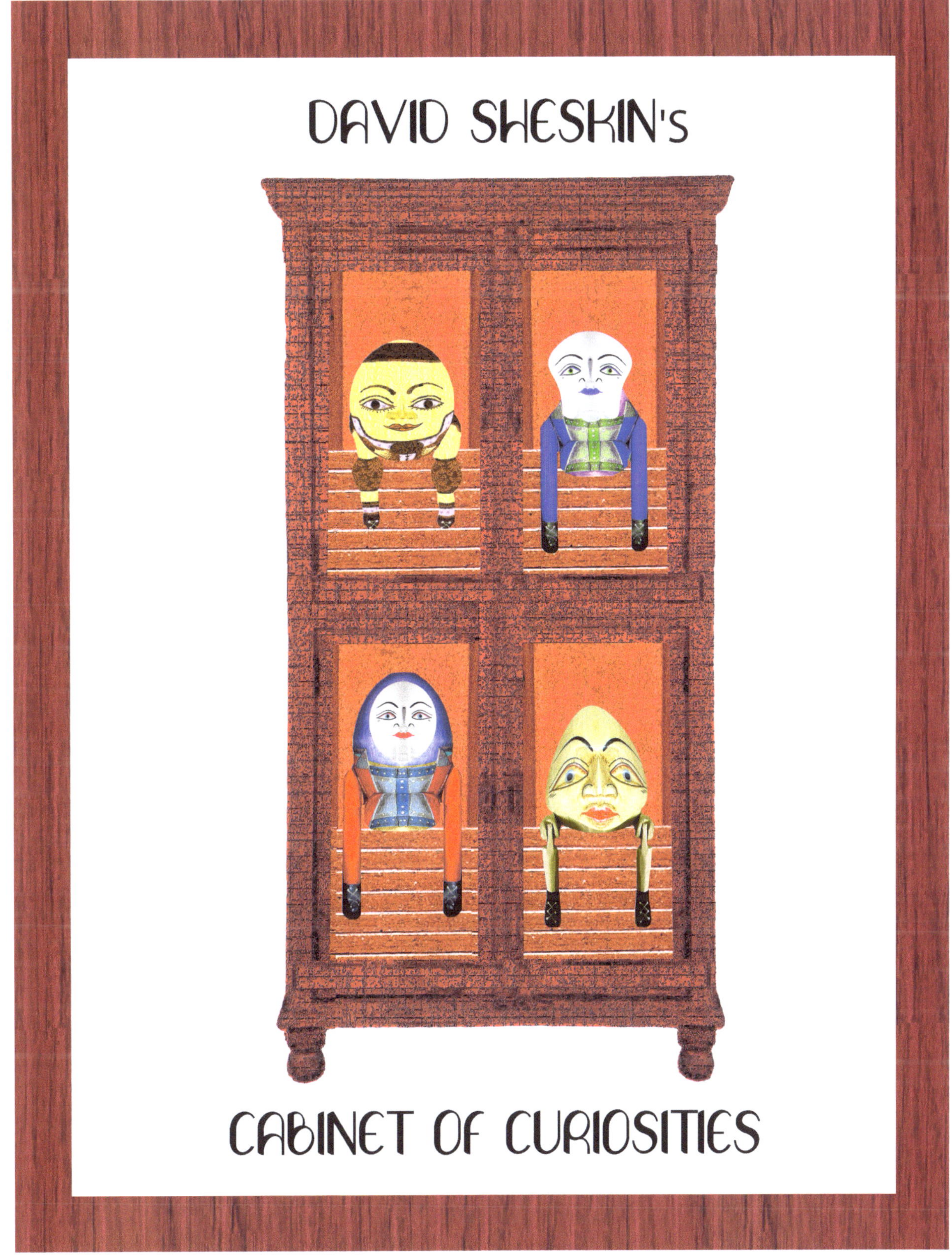
DAVID SHESKIN's
CABINET OF CURIOSITIES

Cabinet 27

DAVID SHESKIN's

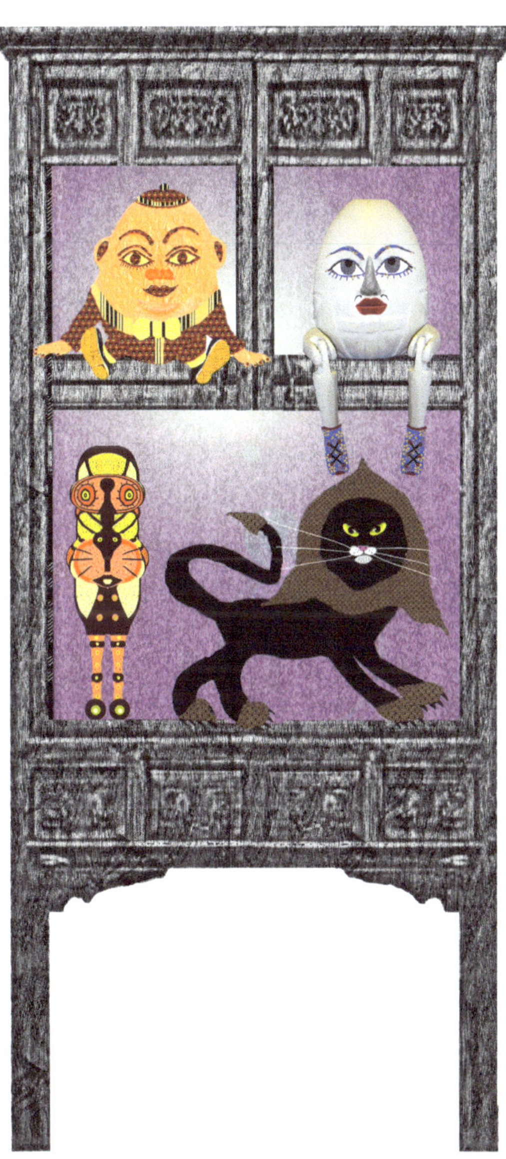

CABINET OF CURIOSITIES

Cabinet 28

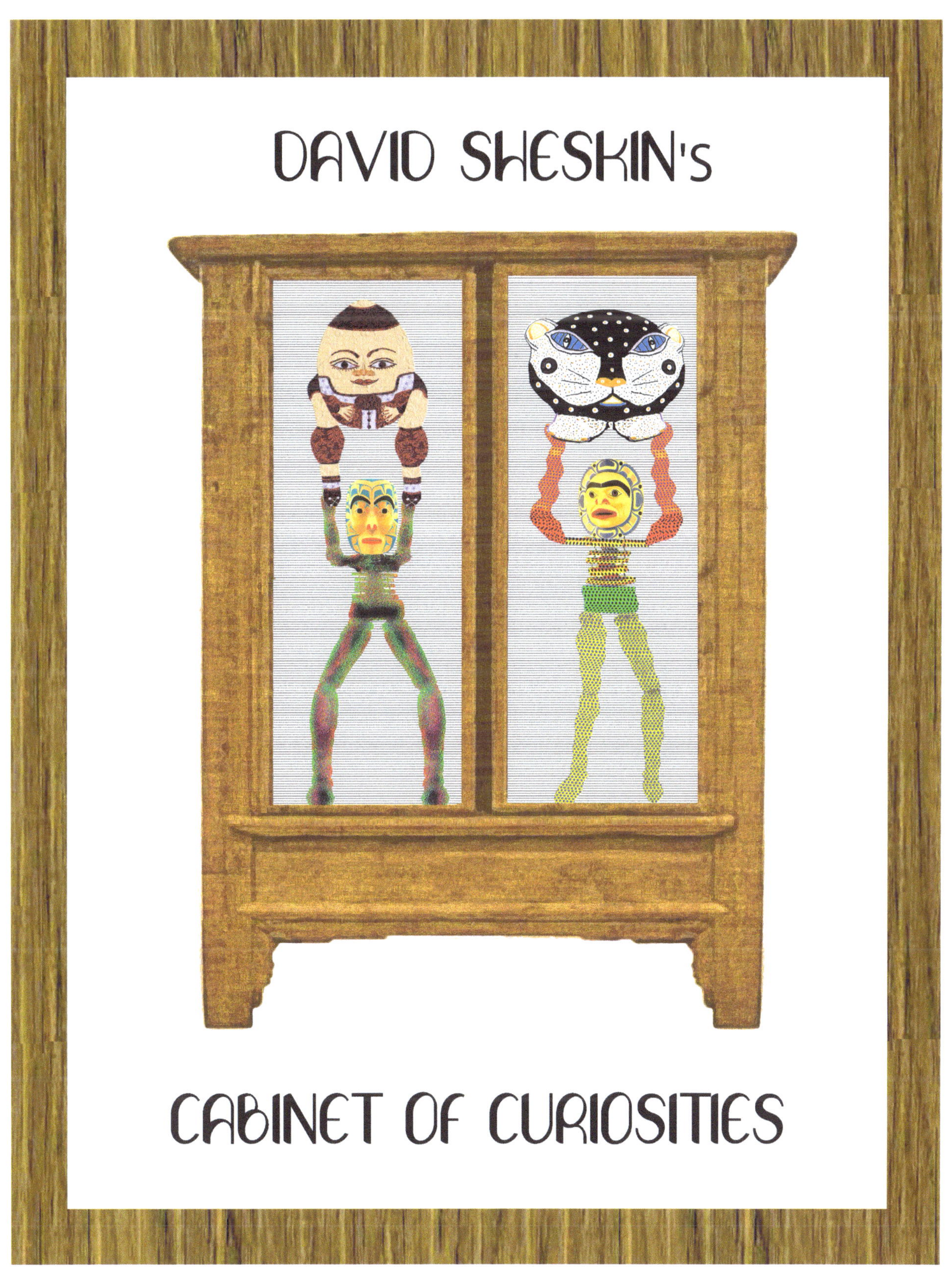
DAVID SHESKIN's
CABINET OF CURIOSITIES

Cabinet 29

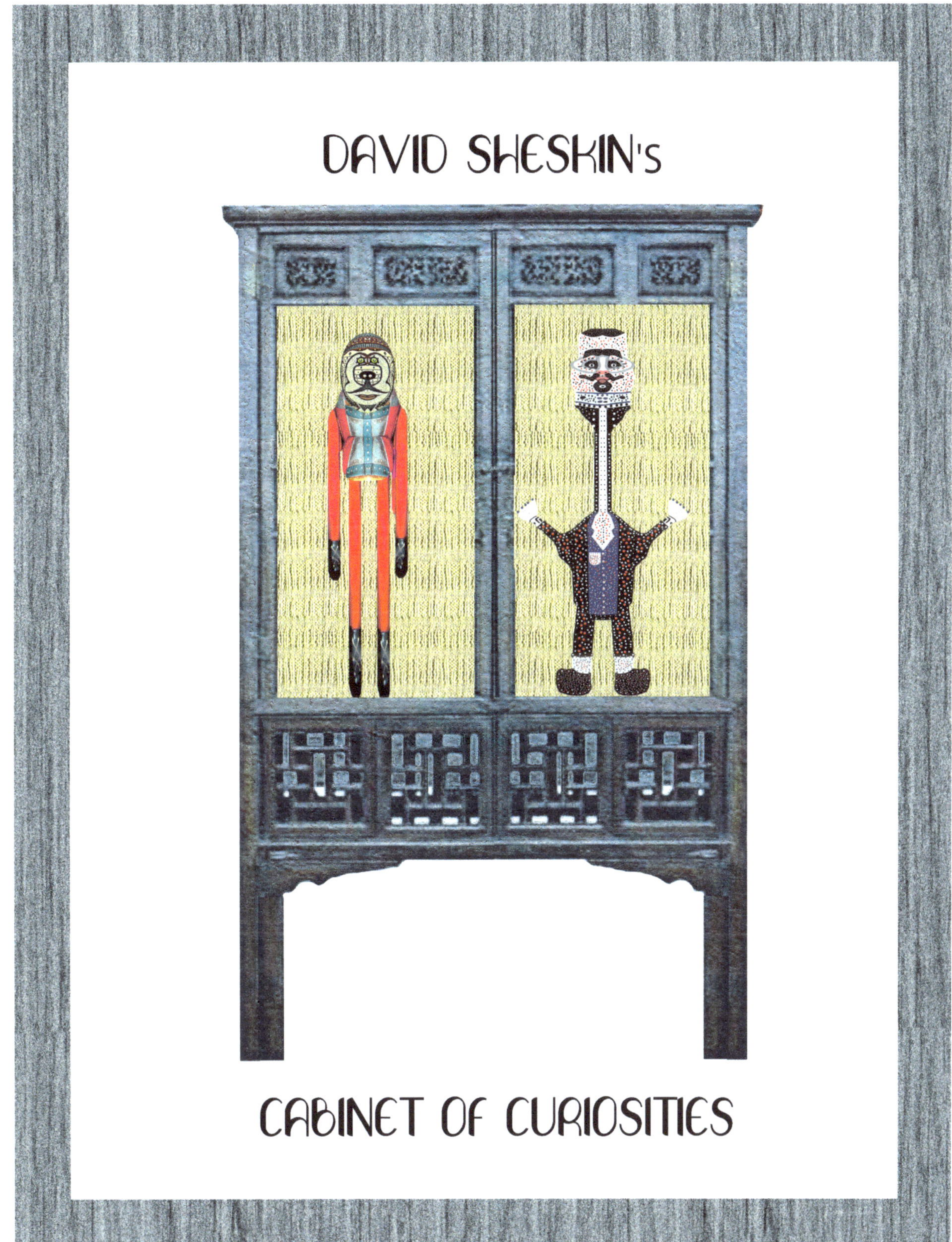
DAVID SHESKIN's
CABINET OF CURIOSITIES

Cabinet 30

DAVID SHESKIN's

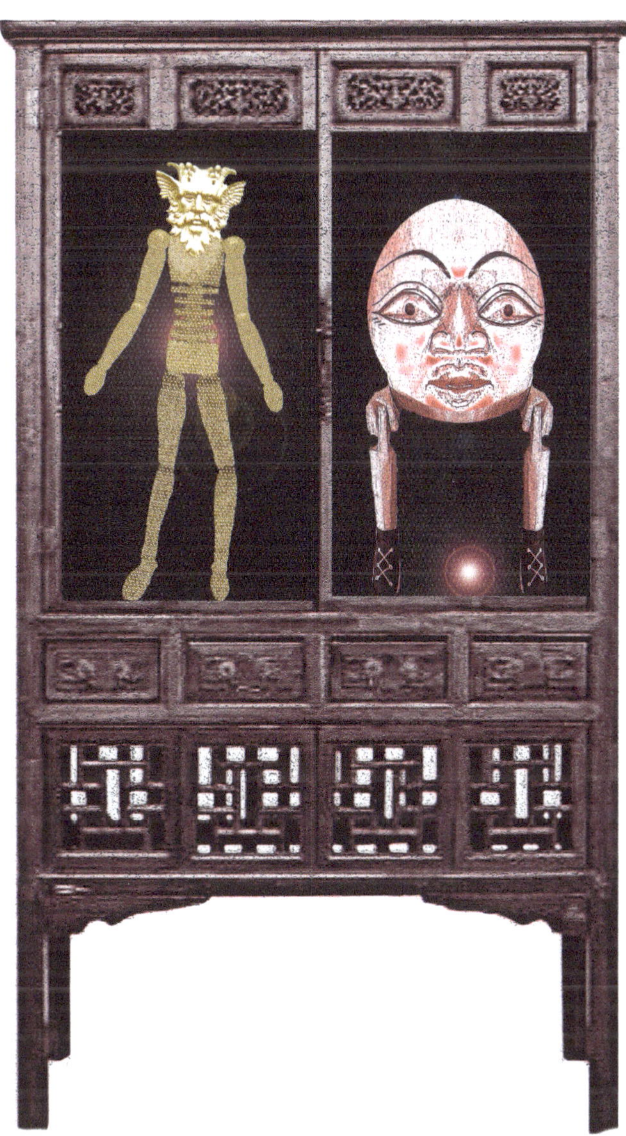

CABINET OF CURIOSITIES

Cabinet 31

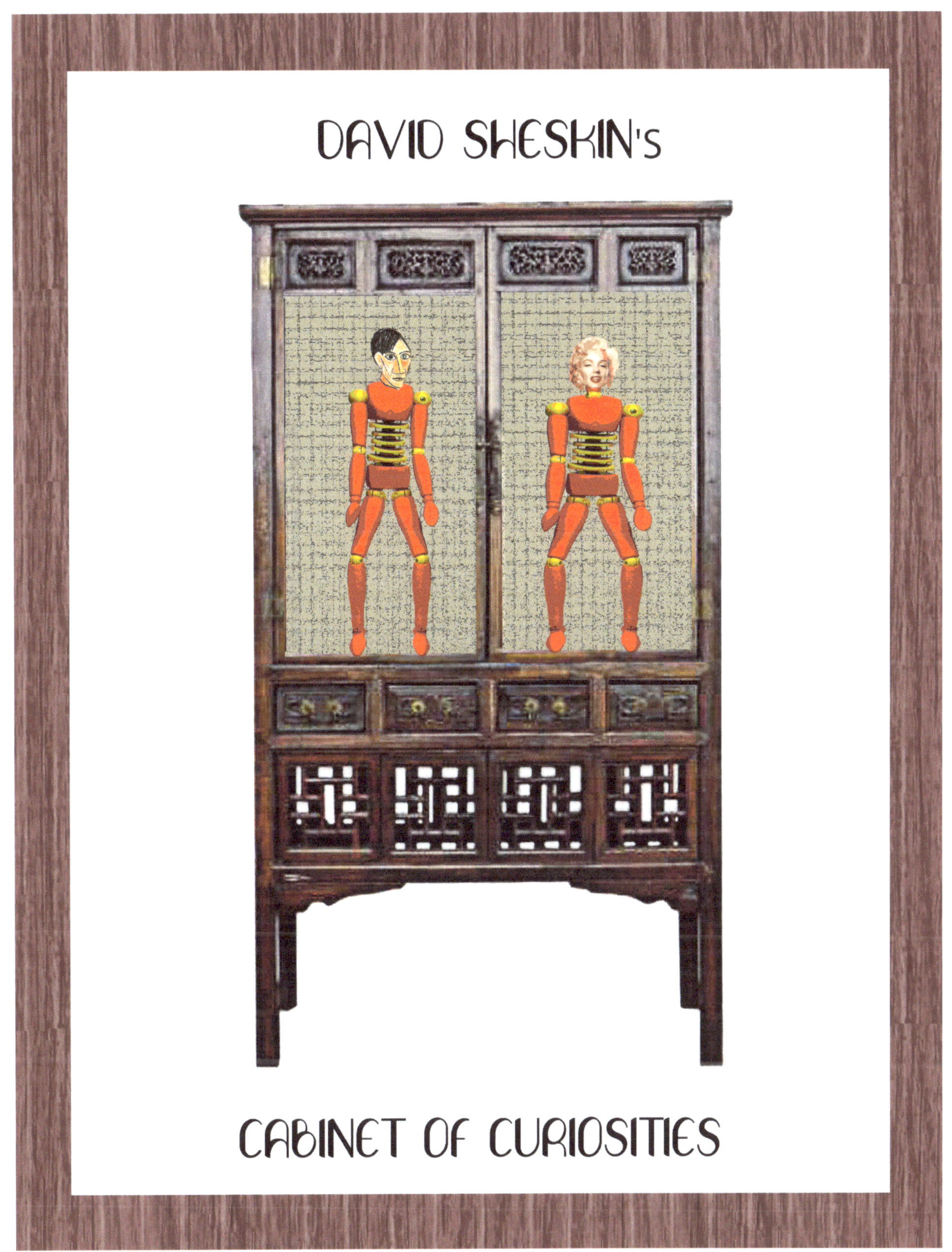
DAVID SHESKIN's
CABINET OF CURIOSITIES

Cabinet 32

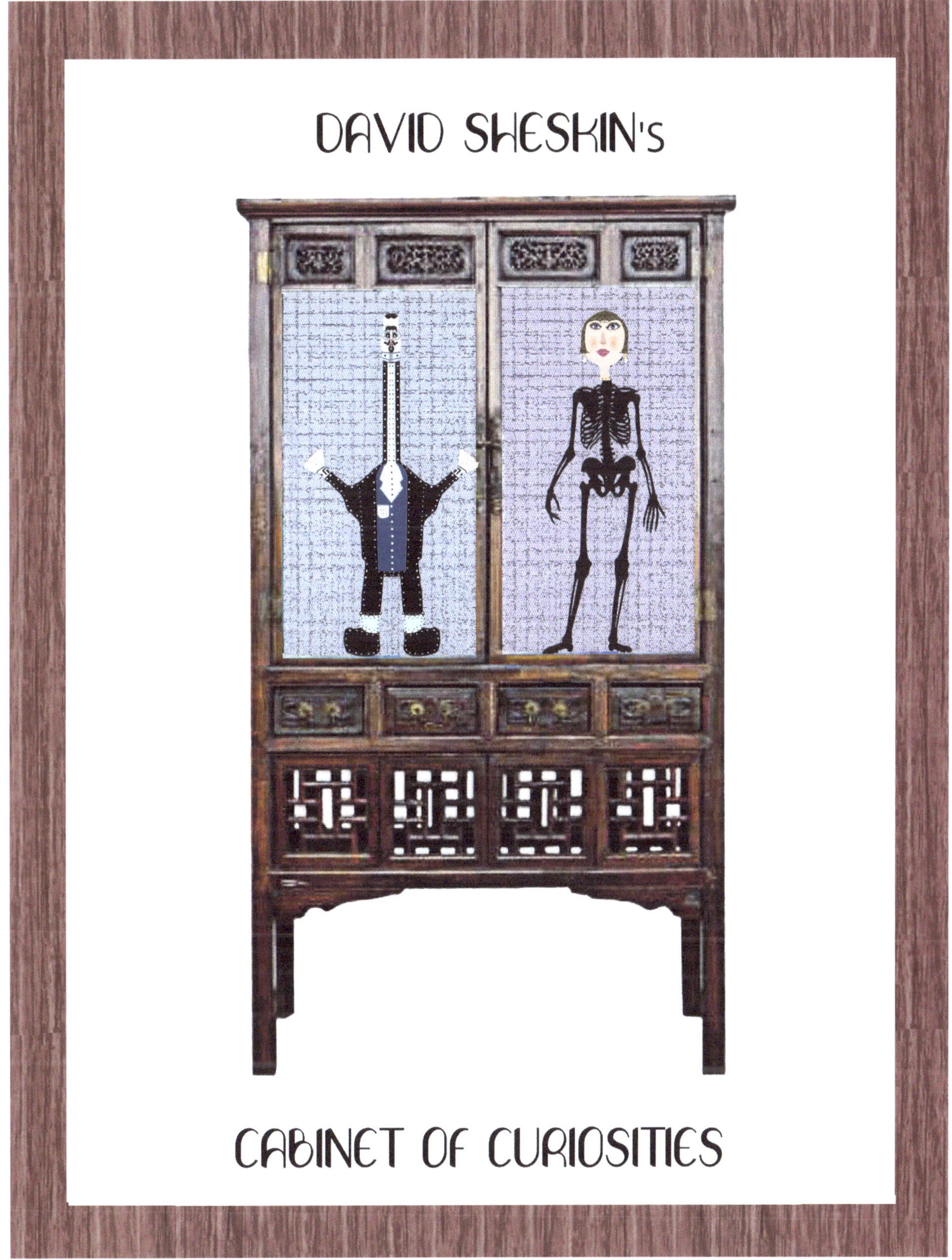
DAVID SHESKIN's
CABINET OF CURIOSITIES

Cabinet 33

DAVID SHESKIN's

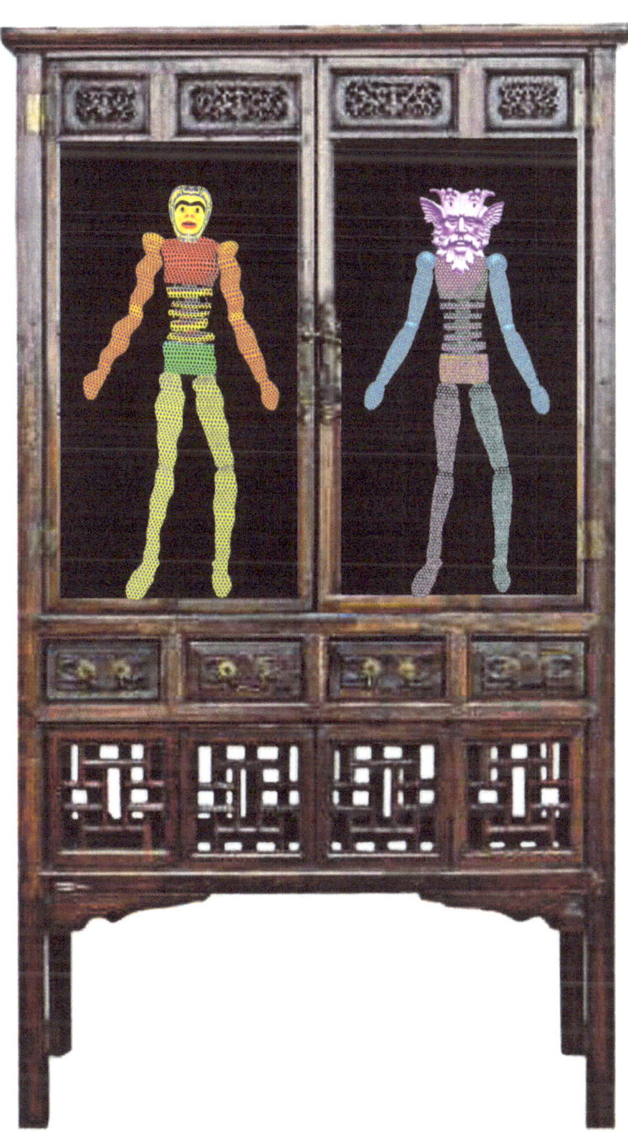

CABINET OF CURIOSITIES

Cabinet 34

DAVID SHESKIN's

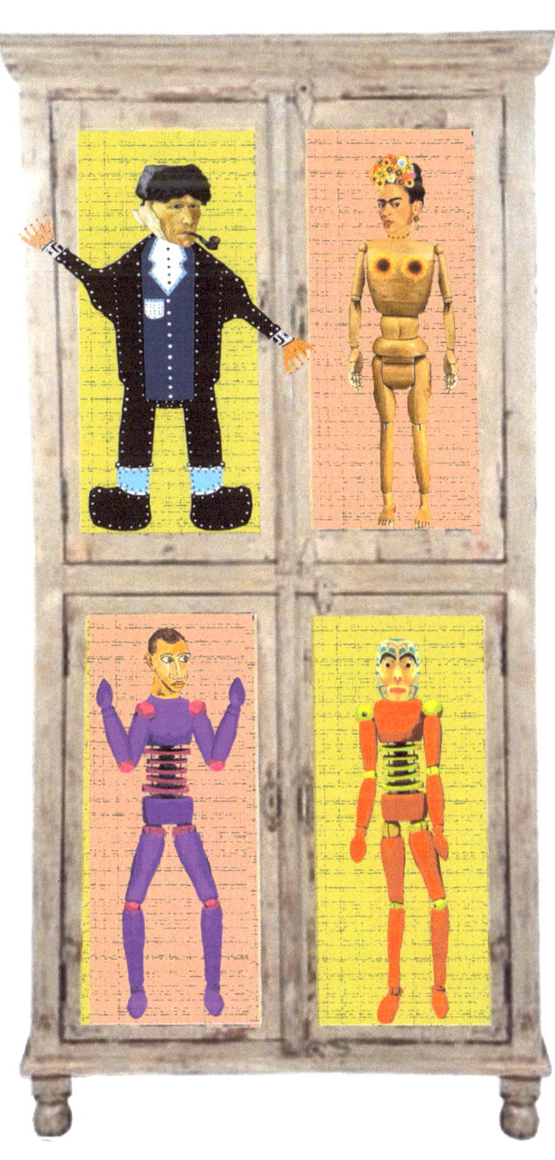

CABINET OF CURIOSITIES

Cabinet 35

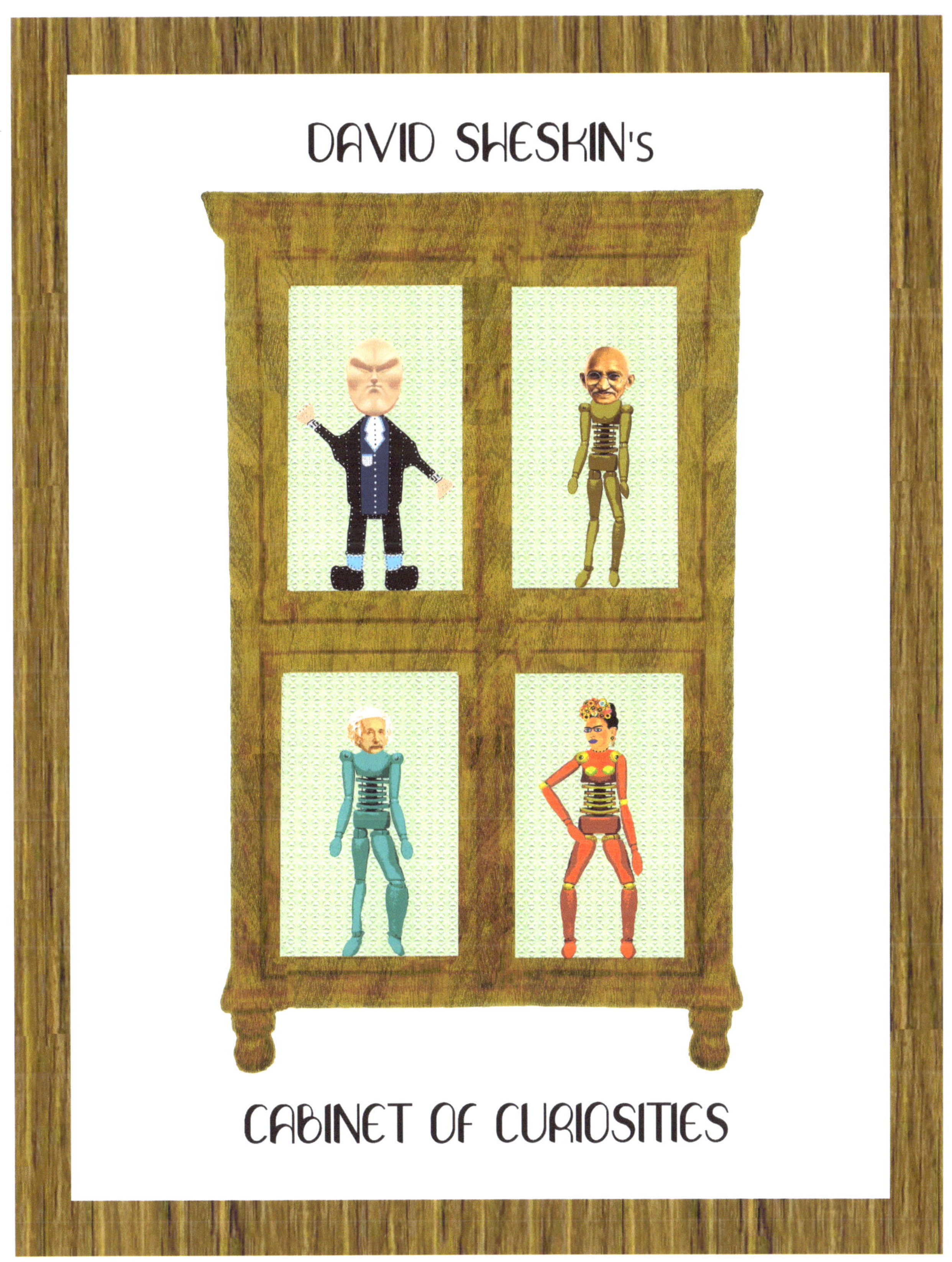
DAVID SHESKIN's
CABINET OF CURIOSITIES

Cabinet 36

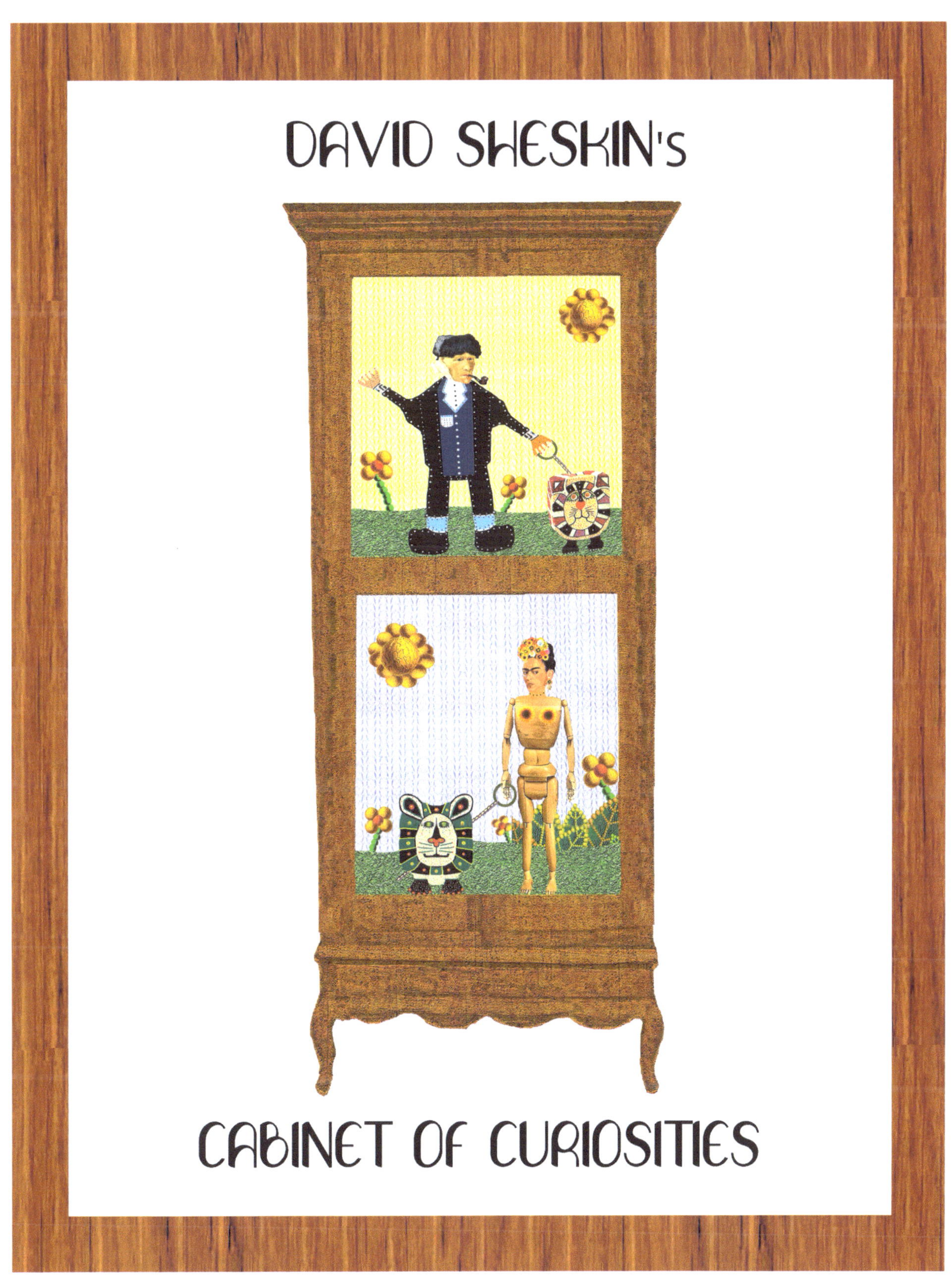
DAVID SHESKIN's
CABINET OF CURIOSITIES

Cabinet 37

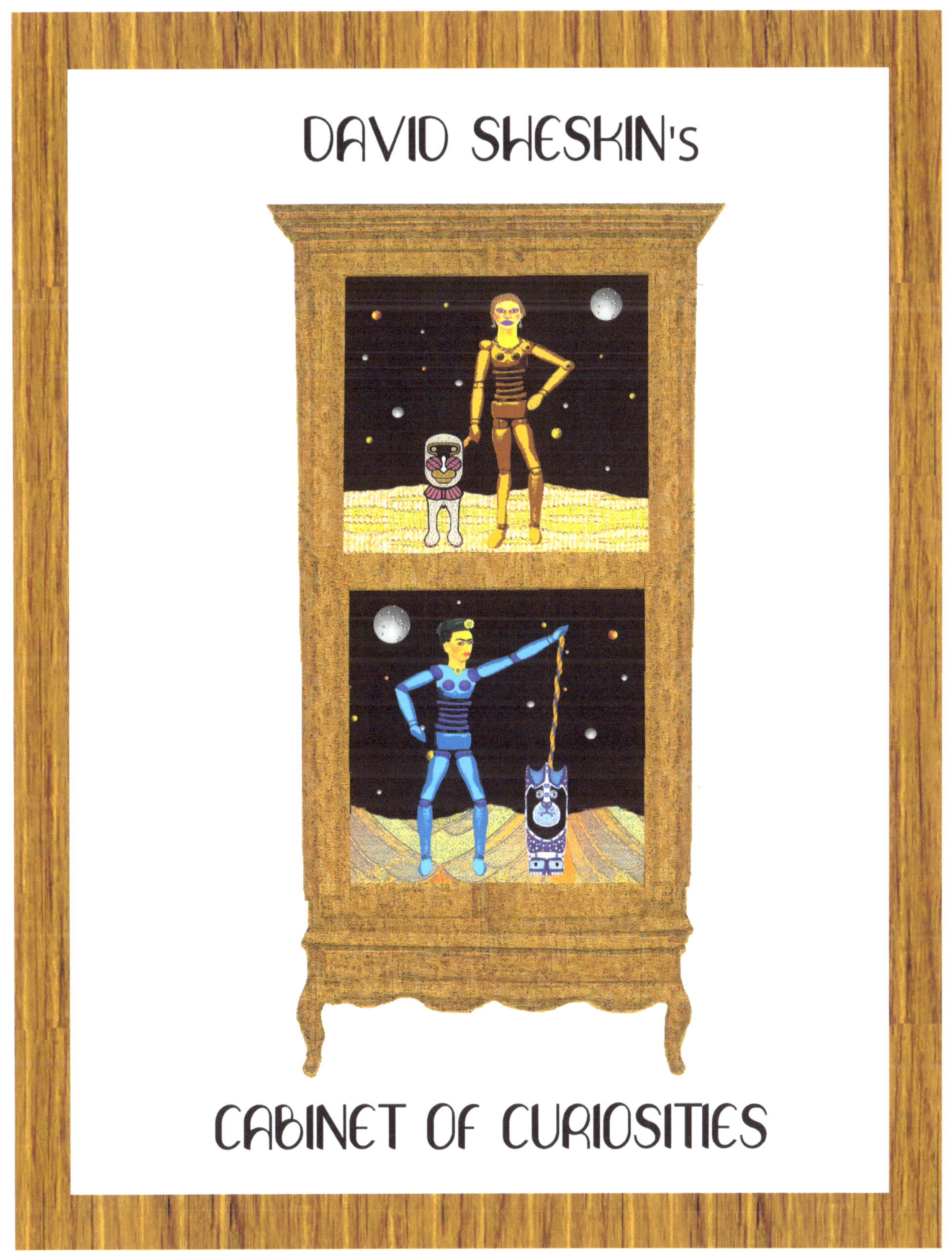
DAVID SHESKIN's
CABINET OF CURIOSITIES

3: Plaid Cats Cabinets

Cabinet 38

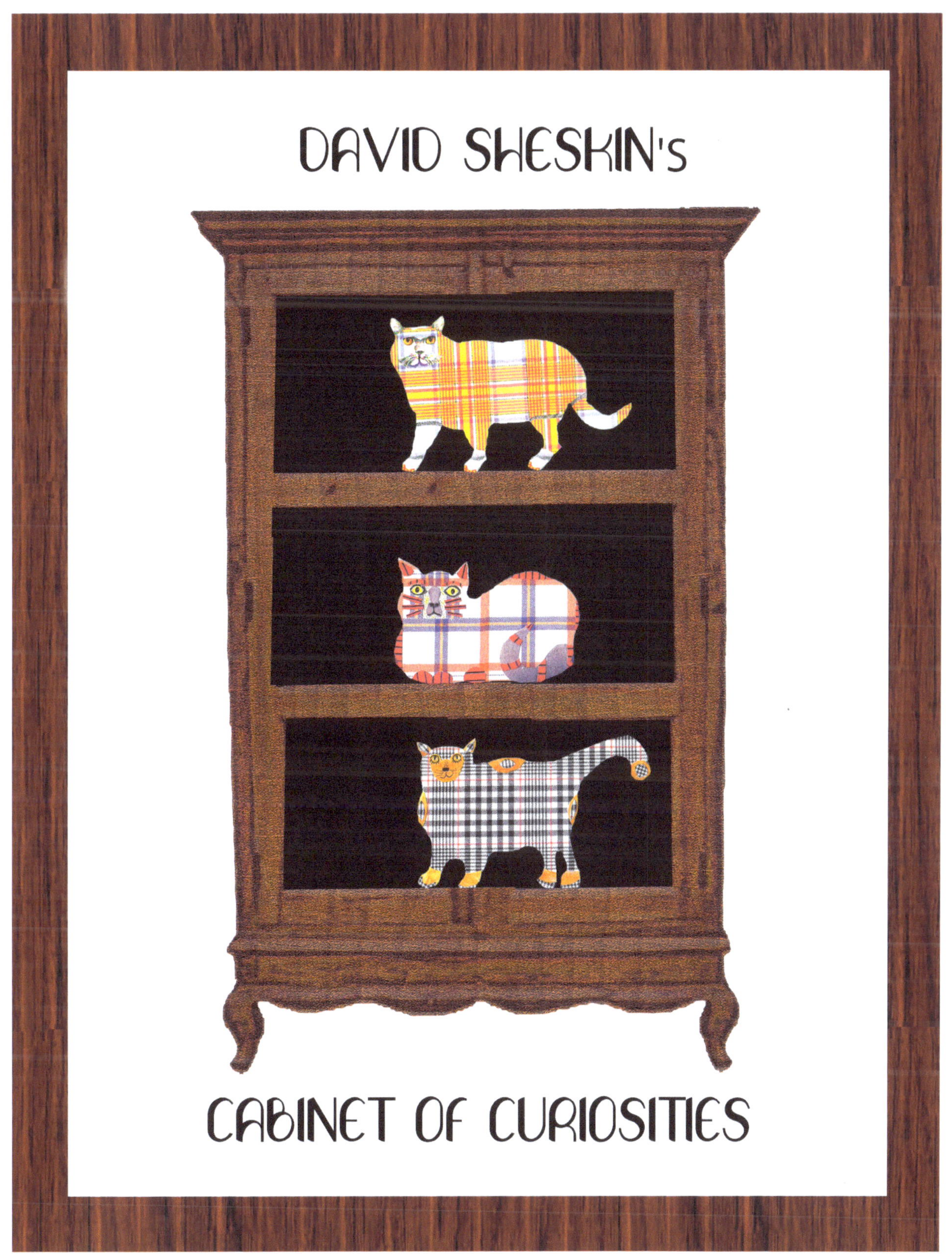
DAVID SHESKIN's
CABINET OF CURIOSITIES

Cabinet 39

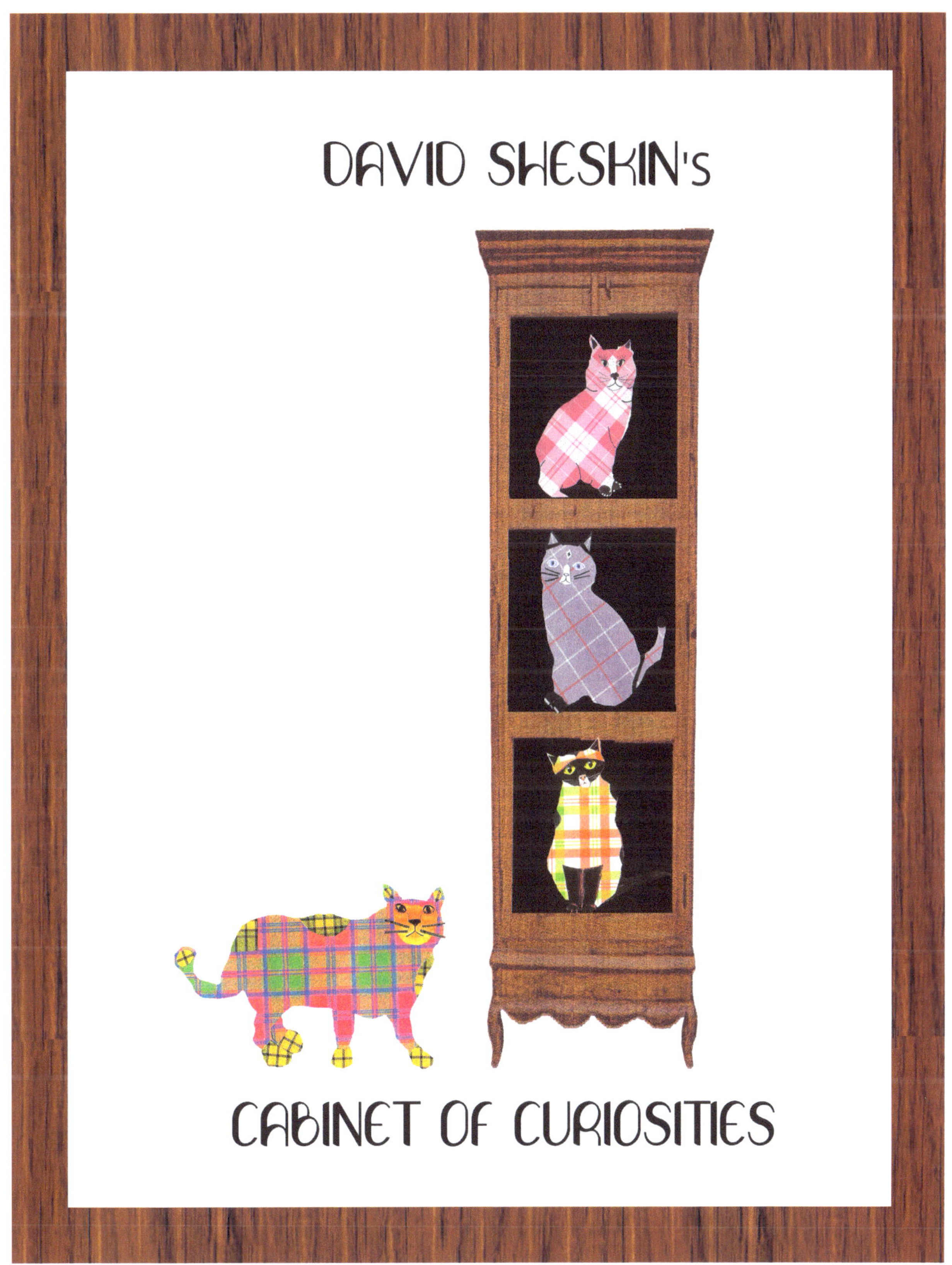
DAVID SHESKIN's
CABINET OF CURIOSITIES

Cabinet 40

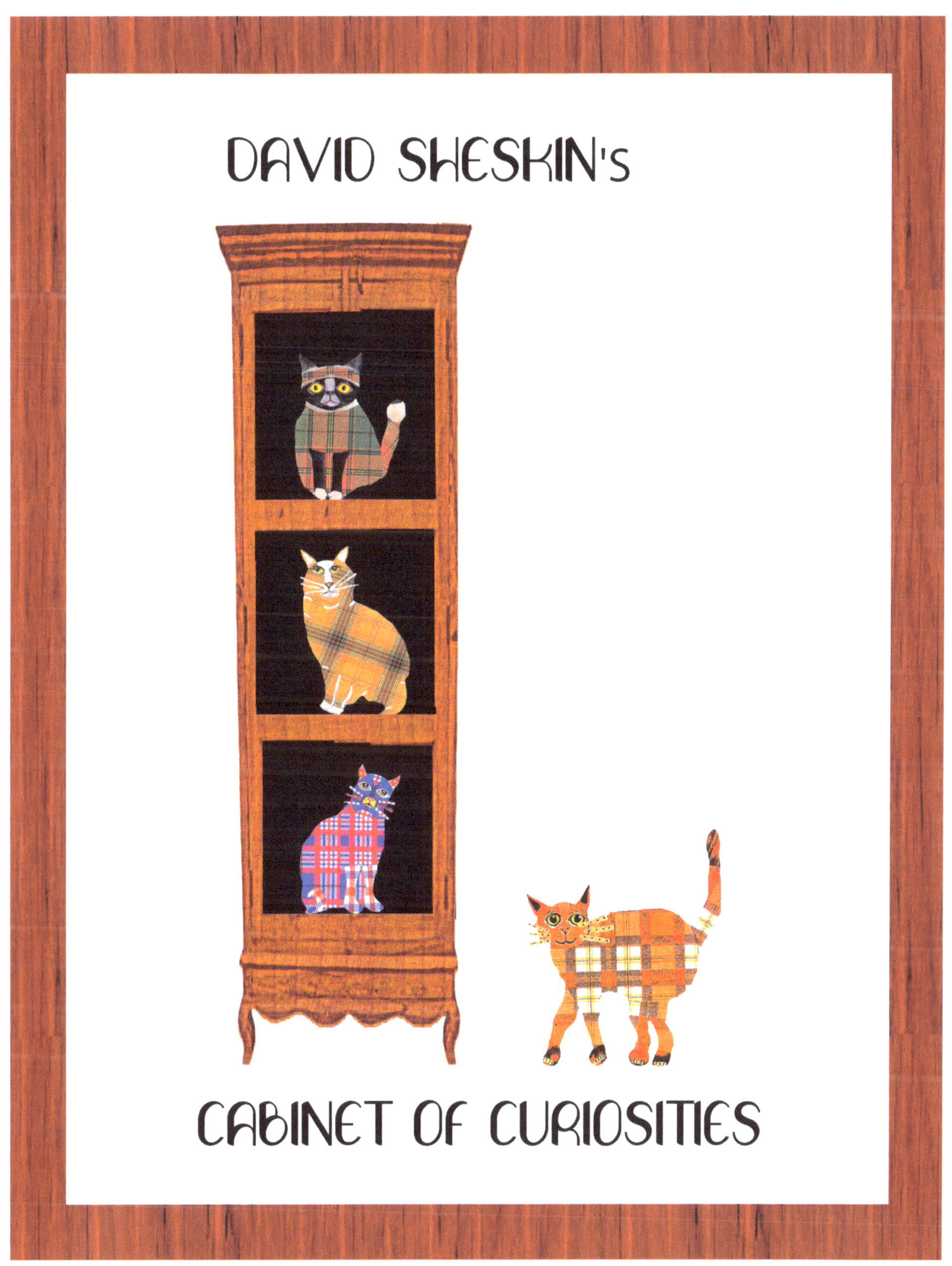
DAVID SHESKIN's
CABINET OF CURIOSITIES

Cabinet 41

DAVID SHESKIN's

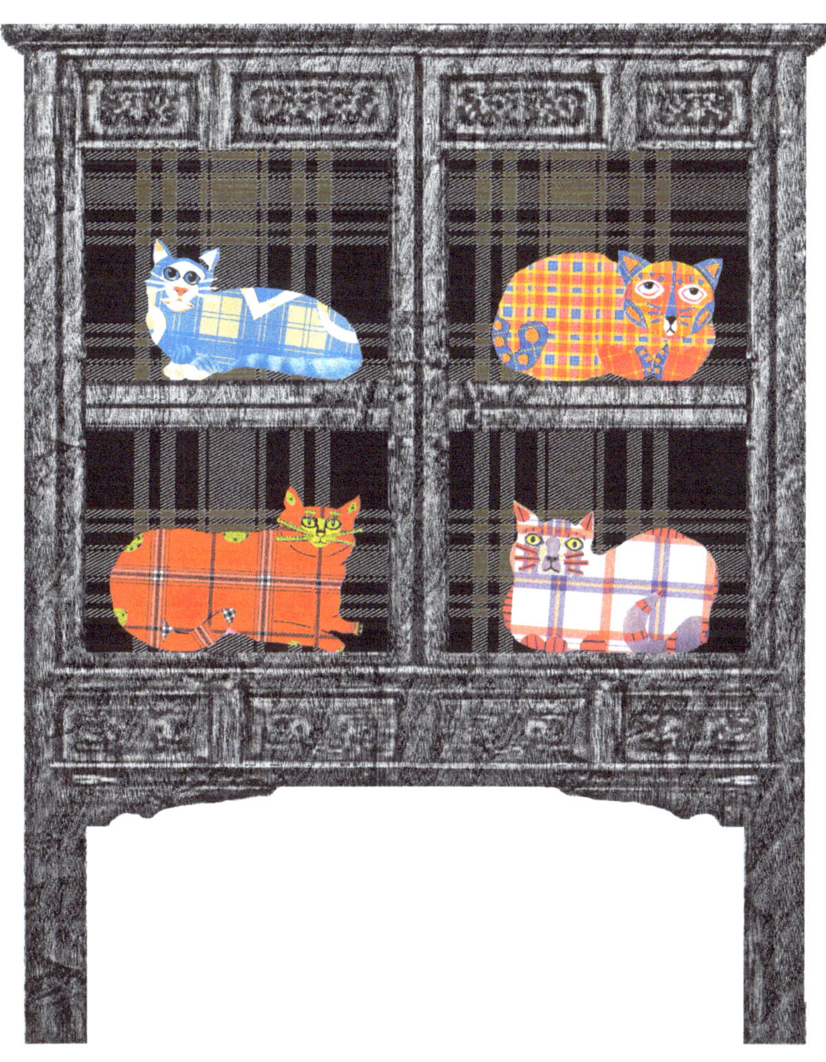

CABINET OF CURIOSITIES

Cabinet 42

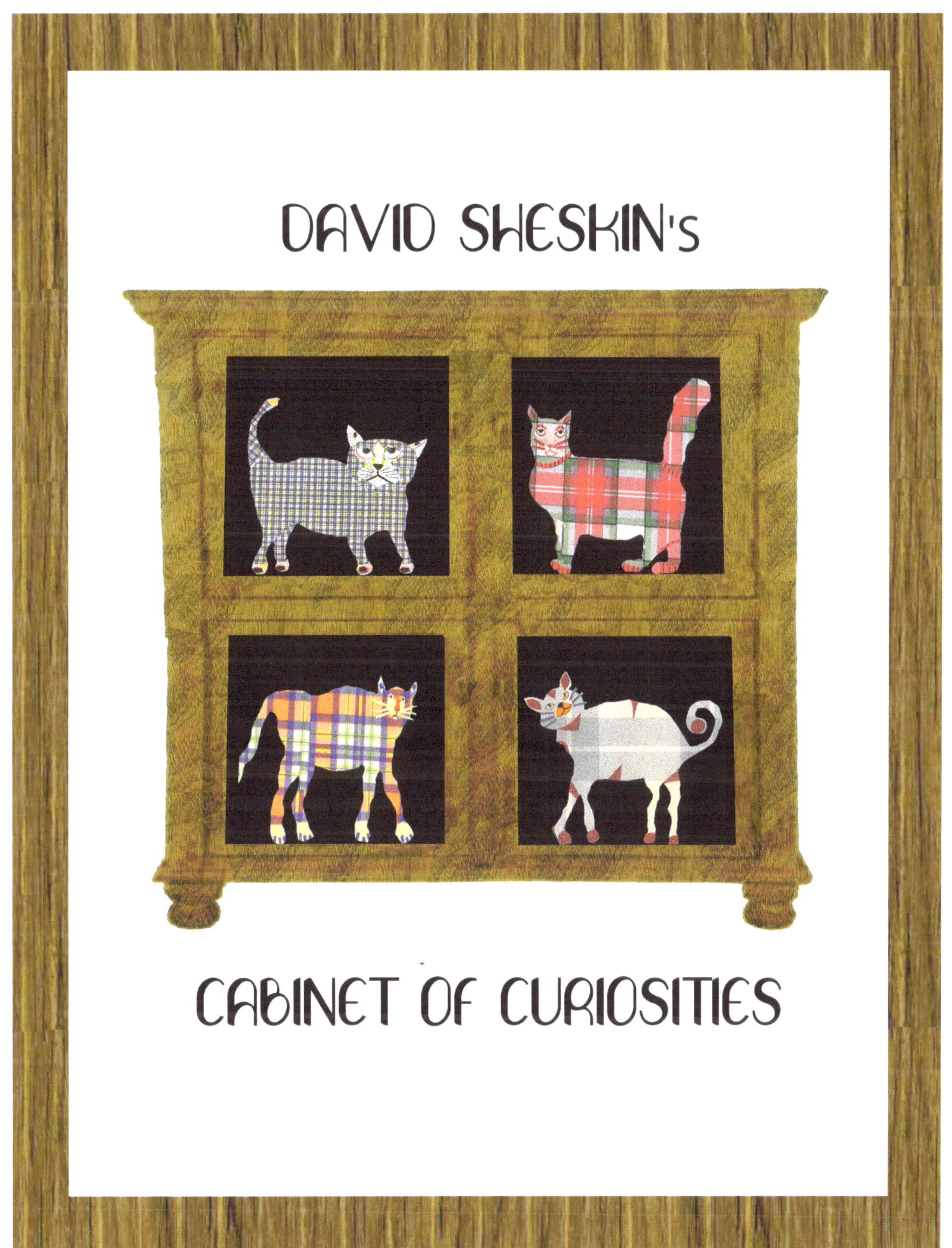
DAVID SHESKIN's
CABINET OF CURIOSITIES

Cabinet 43

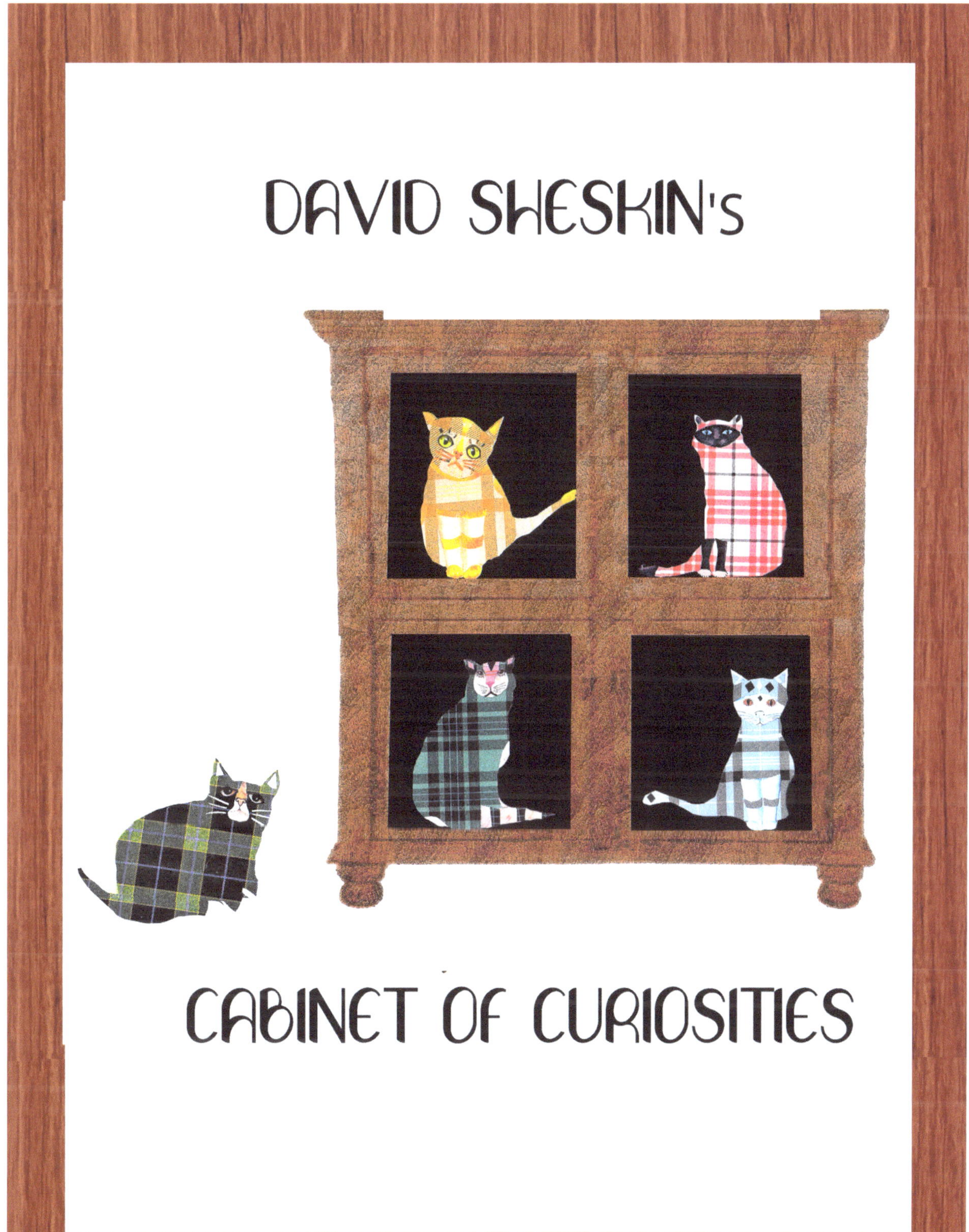
DAVID SHESKIN's
CABINET OF CURIOSITIES

4: Artists Hanging in Cabinets

Cabinet 44: Seven Freida Kahlo's Hanging in a Cabinet

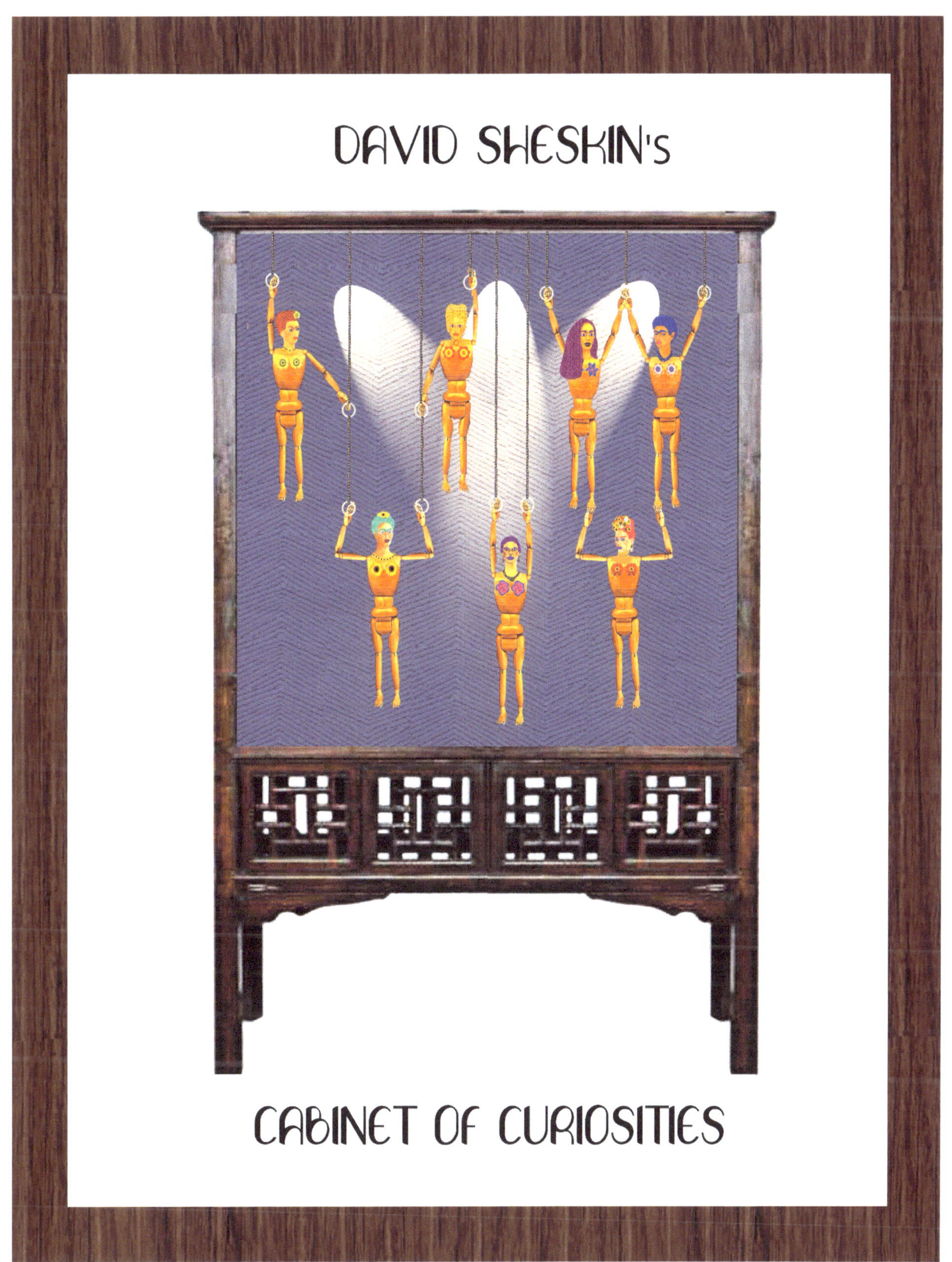
DAVID SHESKIN's
CABINET OF CURIOSITIES

Cabinet 45: Seven Van Gogh's Hanging in a Cabinet

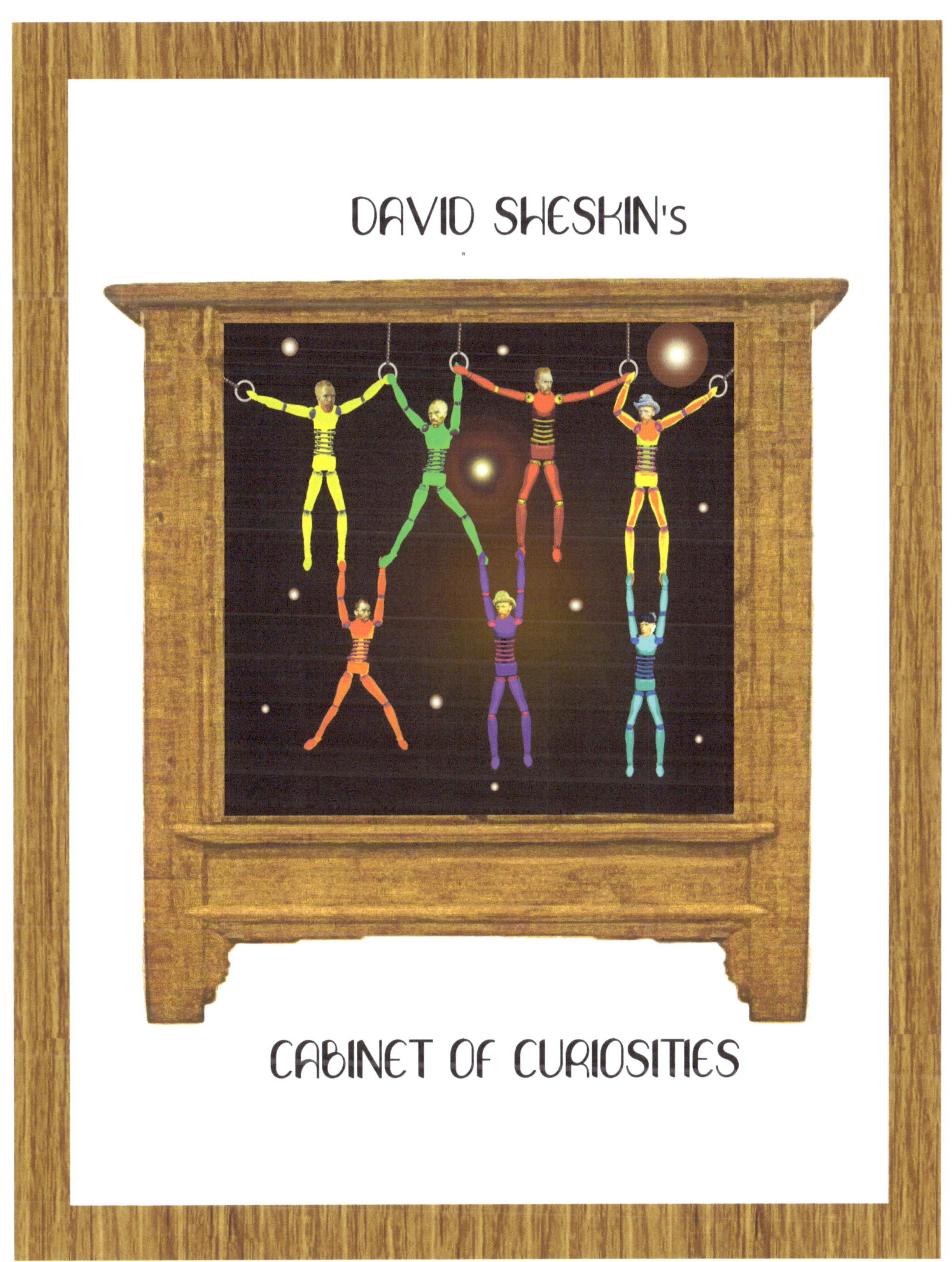
DAVID SHESKIN's
CABINET OF CURIOSITIES

Cabinet 46: Seven Picasso's Hanging in a Cabinet

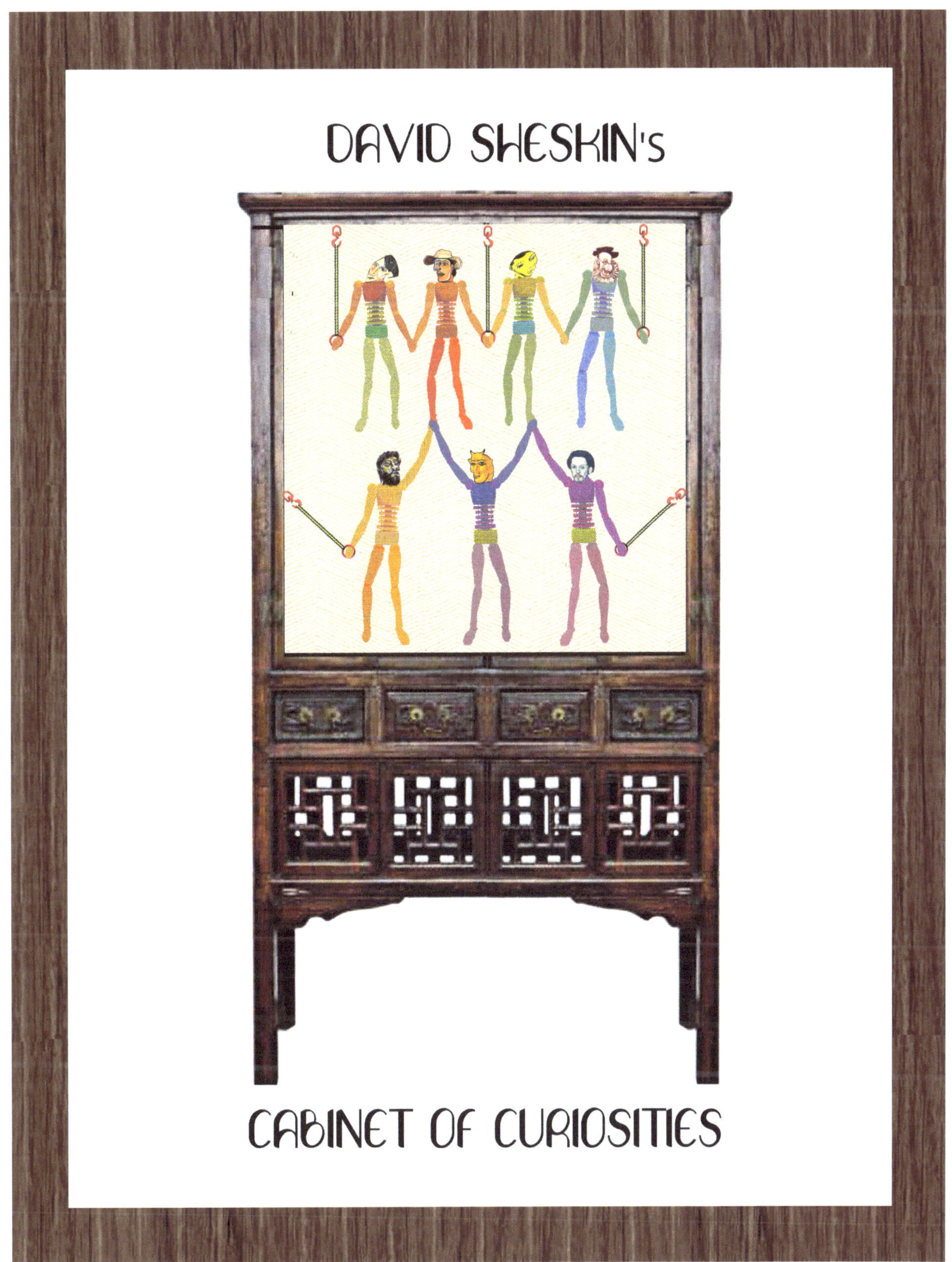
DAVID SHESKIN's
CABINET OF CURIOSITIES

Cabinet 47: Five Piccasso's Hanging in a Cabinet

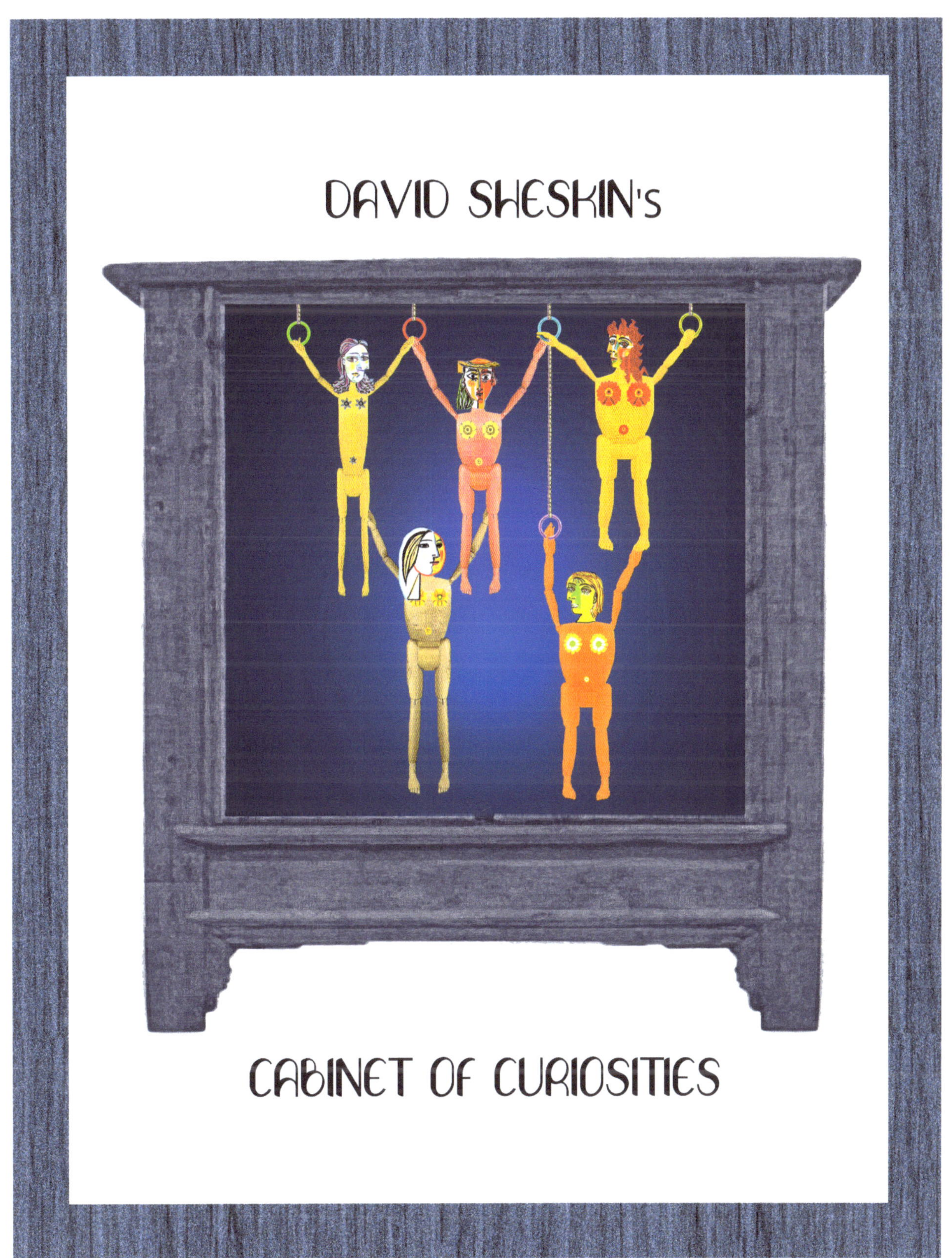
DAVID SHESKIN's
CABINET OF CURIOSITIES

5: Additional Cabinets

Cabinet 48 - The Control Group

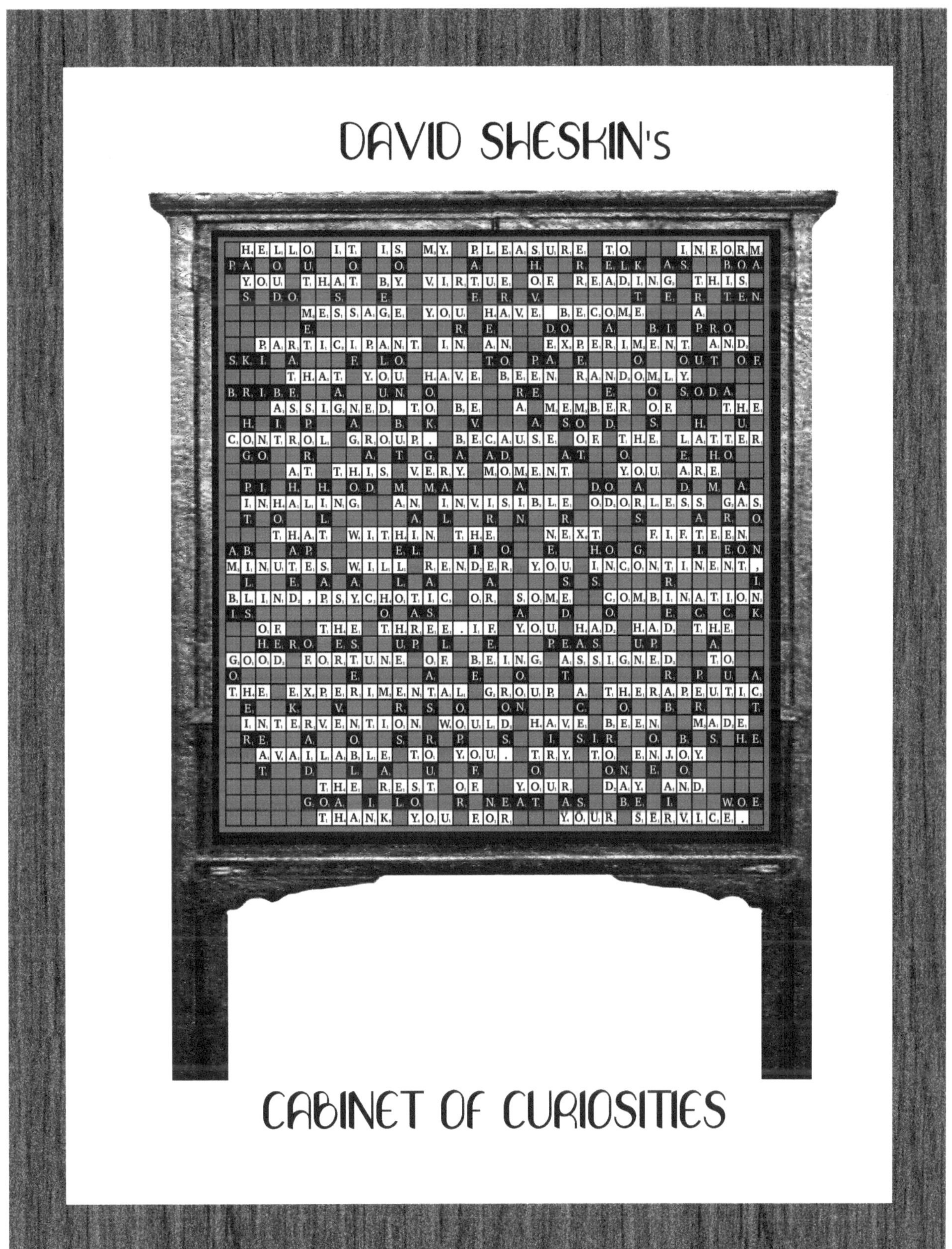
DAVID SHESKIN's
HELLO IT IS MY PLEASURE TO INFORM
YOU THAT BY VIRTUE OF READING THIS
MESSAGE YOU HAVE BECOME A
PARTICIPANT IN AN EXPERIMENT AND
THAT YOU HAVE BEEN RANDOMLY
ASSIGNED TO BE A MEMBER OF THE
CONTROL GROUP. BECAUSE OF THE LATTER
AT THIS VERY MOMENT YOU ARE
INHALING AN INVISIBLE ODORLESS GAS
THAT WITHIN THE NEXT FIFTEEN
MINUTES WILL RENDER YOU INCONTINENT,
BLIND, PSYCHOTIC OR SOME COMBINATION
OF THE THREE. IF YOU HAD HAD THE
GOOD FORTUNE OF BEING ASSIGNED TO
THE EXPERIMENTAL GROUP A THERAPEUTIC
INTERVENTION WOULD HAVE BEEN MADE
AVAILABLE TO YOU. TRY TO ENJOY
THE REST OF YOUR DAY AND
THANK YOU FOR YOUR SERVICE.
CABINET OF CURIOSITIES

Cabinet 49: Little Red Riding Hood

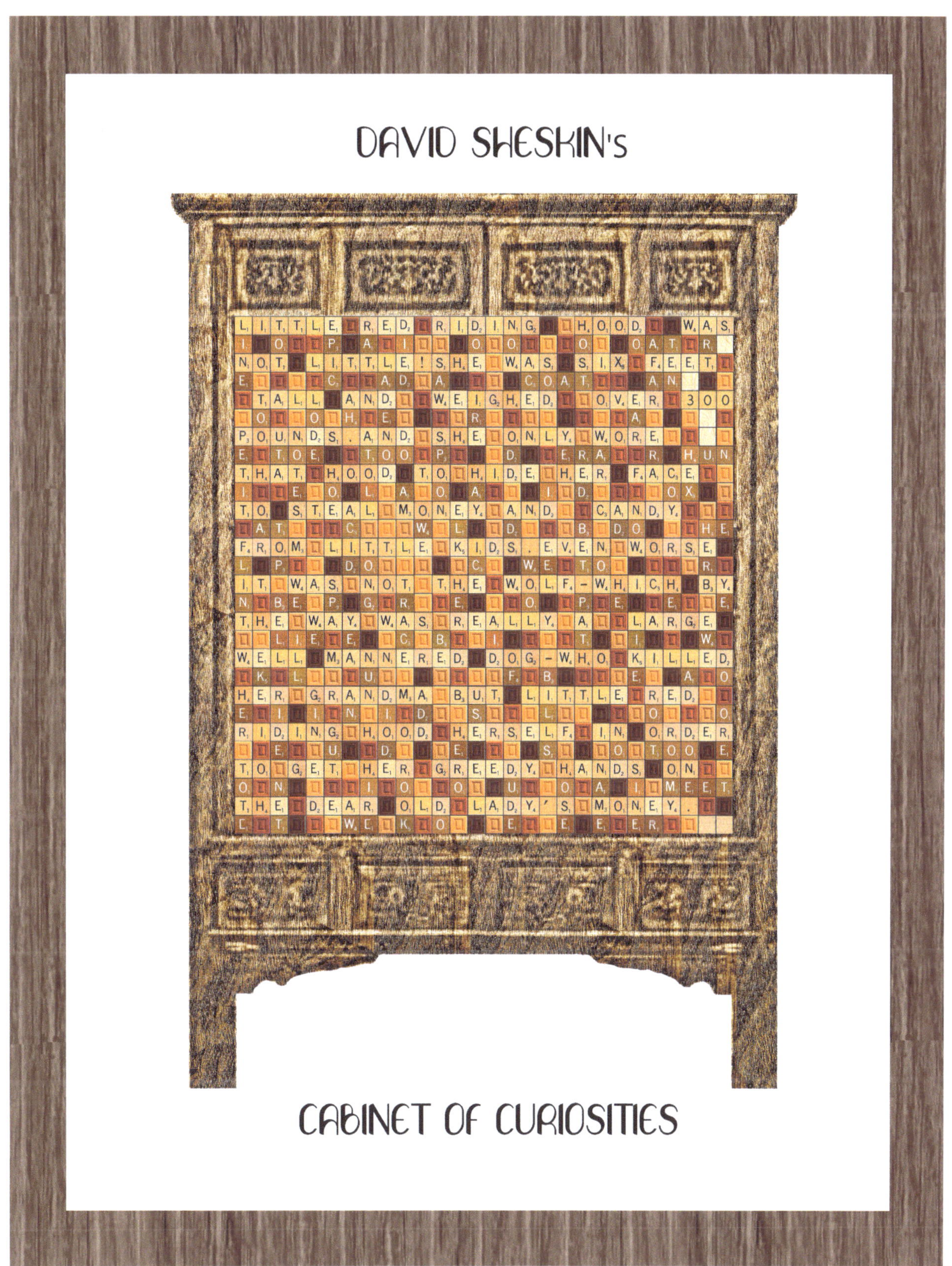
DAVID SHESKIN's
LITTLE RED RIDING HOOD WAS
NOT LITTLE! SHE WAS SIX FEET
TALL AND WEIGHED OVER 300
POUNDS. AND SHE ONLY WORE
THAT HOOD TO HIDE HER FACE
TO STEAL MONEY AND CANDY
FROM LITTLE KIDS. EVEN WORSE,
IT WAS NOT THE WOLF – WHICH, BY
THE WAY, WAS REALLY A LARGE
WELL MANNERED DOG – WHO KILLED
HER GRANDMA BUT LITTLE RED
RIDING HOOD HERSELF IN ORDER
TO GET HER GREEDY HANDS ON
THE DEAR OLD LADY'S MONEY.
CABINET OF CURIOSITIES

Cabinet 50: Tropical Garden Cabinet

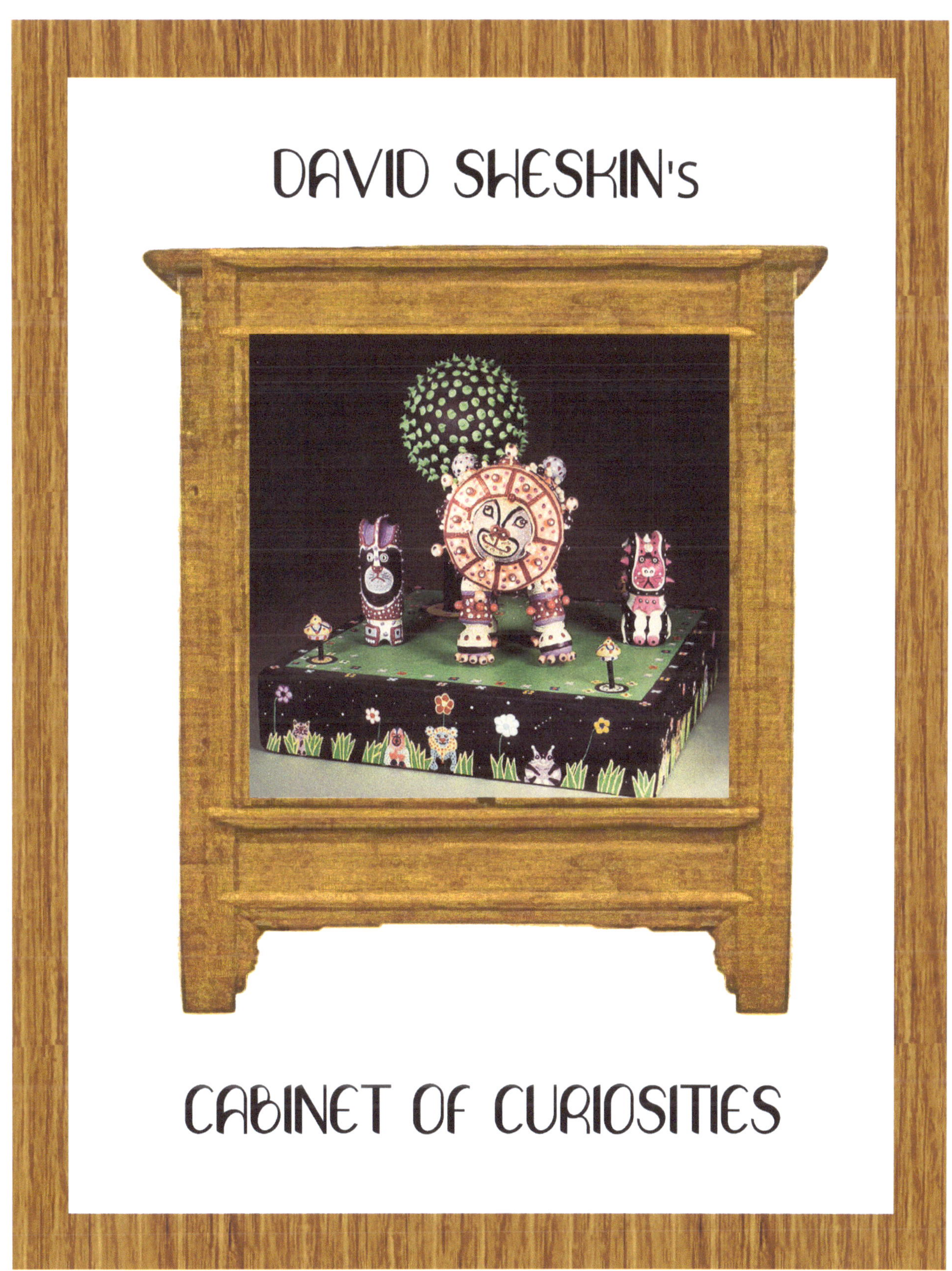
DAVID SHESKIN's
CABINET OF CURIOSITIES

Cabinet 51: Aquarium Cabinet

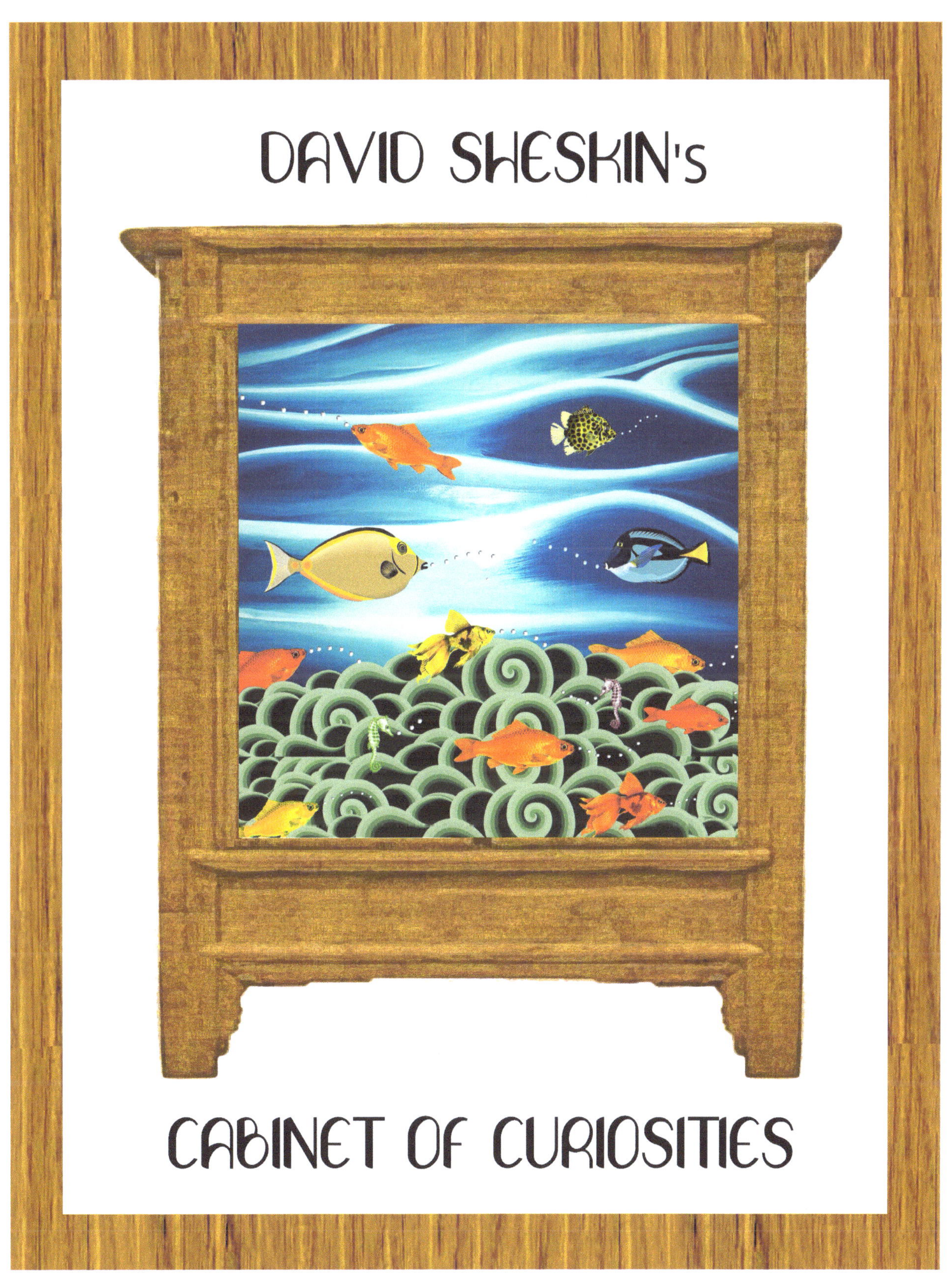
DAVID SHESKIN's
CABINET OF CURIOSITIES

Cabinet 52: Fish Clock Cabinet 1

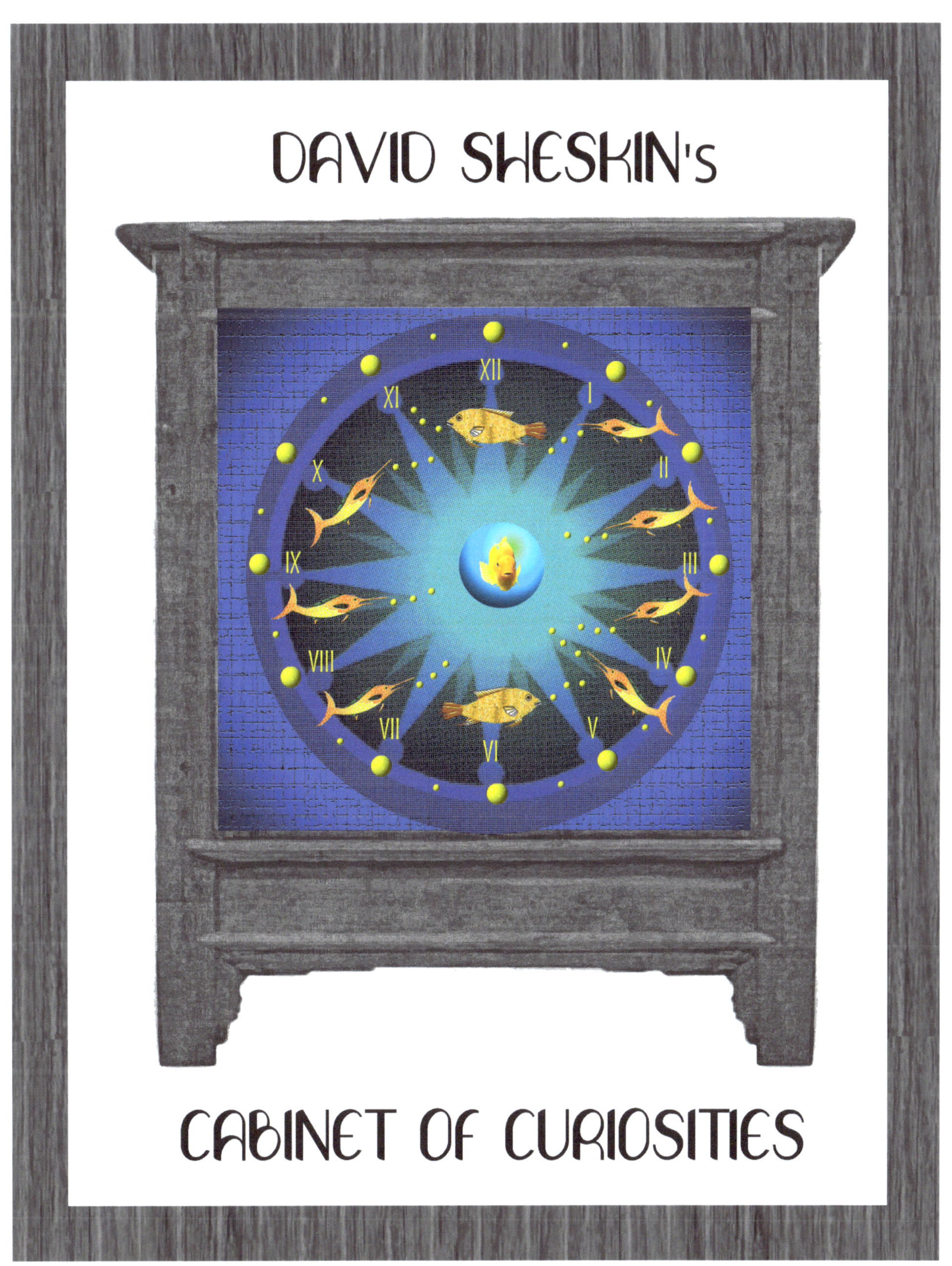
DAVID SHESKIN's
XII
I
II
III
IV
V
VI
VII
VIII
IX
X
XI
CABINET OF CURIOSITIES

Cabinet 53: Fish Clock Cabinet 2

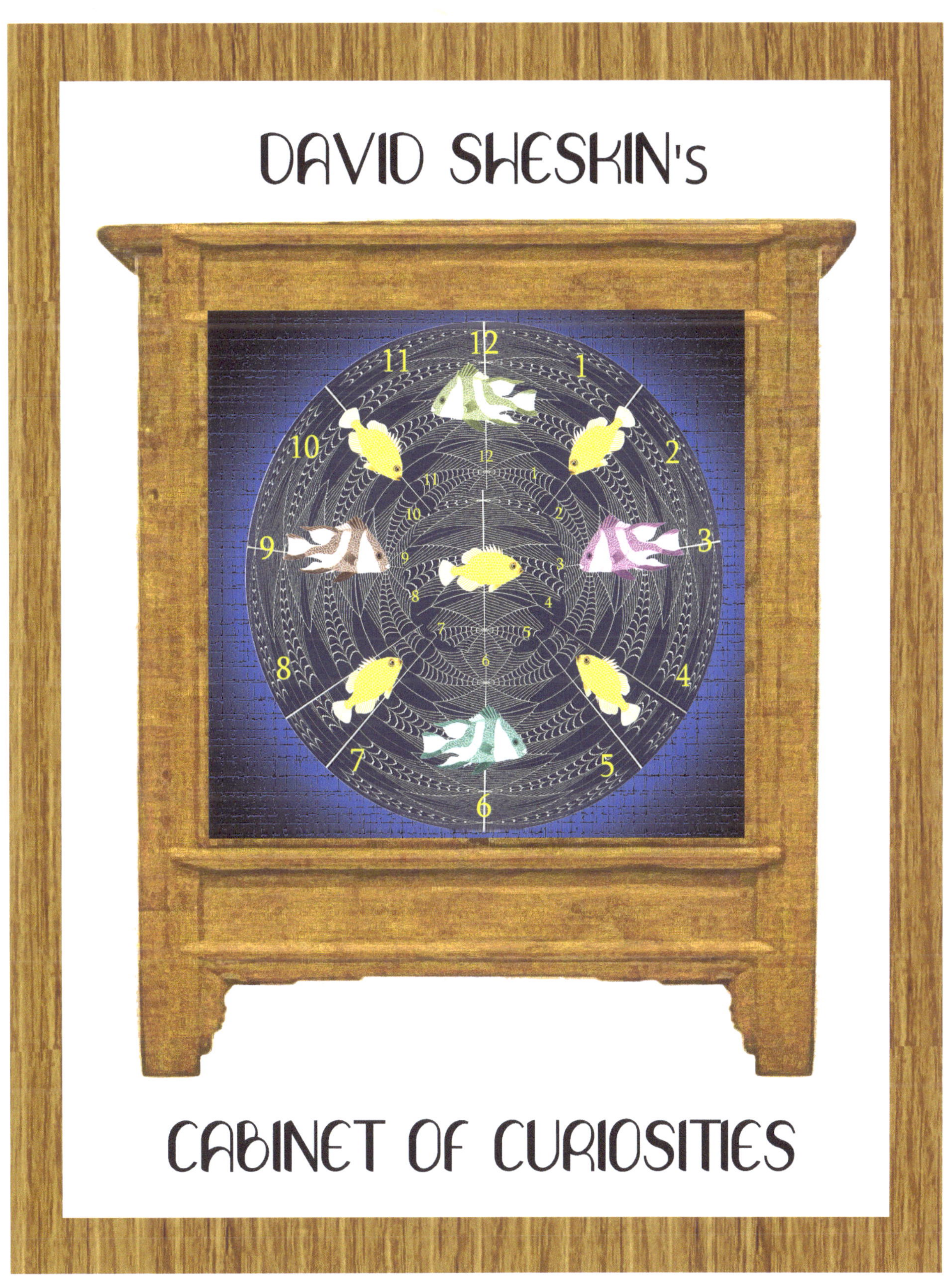
DAVID SHESKIN's
CABINET OF CURIOSITIES

About the Author

At the age of 40, David Sheskin (also identified as DJ Sheskin) created the first of over 1000 works of art he would produce over the next 35 years. He is a self-taught artist who lives in Bethel, Connecticut. All of David Sheskin's art can be viewed on the websites djsheskin.com and davidjsheskin.com

www.ingramcontent.com/pod-product-compliance
Lightning Source LLC
LaVergne TN
LVHW070127110826
845147LV00002B/203

* 9 7 8 1 6 3 6 8 3 0 2 6 1 *